**BLACK+DECKER**

# WOOD FLOORS

Hardwood • Laminate • Bamboo • Wood Tile • and More

MINNEAPOLIS, MINNESOTA

Quarto is the authority on a wide range of topics.
Quarto educates, entertains and enriches the lives of our readers—enthusiasts and lovers of hands-on living.
www.quartoknows.com

© 2017 Quarto Publishing Group USA Inc.

First published in 2017 by Cool Springs Press, an imprint of The Quarto Group, 401 Second Avenue North, Suite 310, Minneapolis, MN 55401 USA. Telephone: (612) 344-8100 Fax: (612) 344-8692

quartoknows.com
Visit our blogs at quartoknows.com

All rights reserved. No part of this book may be reproduced in any form without written permission of the copyright owners. All images in this book have been reproduced with the knowledge and prior consent of the artists concerned, and no responsibility is accepted by producer, publisher, or printer for any infringement of copyright or otherwise, arising from the contents of this publication. Every effort has been made to ensure that credits accurately comply with information supplied. We apologize for any inaccuracies that may have occurred and will resolve inaccurate or missing information in a subsequent reprinting of the book.

Cool Springs Press titles are also available at discount for retail, wholesale, promotional, and bulk purchase. For details, contact the Special Sales Manager by email at specialsales@quarto.com or by mail at The Quarto Group, Attn: Special Sales Manager, 401 Second Avenue North, Suite 310, Minneapolis, MN 55401 USA.

10 9 8 7 6 5 4 3 2 1

ISBN: 978-1-59186-680-0
Digital edition: 978-0-76035-820-7
Softcover edition: 978-1-59186-680-0

Library of Congress Cataloging-in-Publication Data

Names: Black & Decker Corporation (Towson, Md.)
Title: Wood floors : hardwood - laminate - bamboo - wood tile - more.
Other titles: Black & Decker wood floors
Description: Minneapolis : Cool Springs Press, 2017.
Identifiers: LCCN 2016049577 | ISBN 9781591866800 (paperback)
Subjects: LCSH: Floors, Wooden--Amateurs' manuals. | BISAC: HOUSE & HOME / Do-It-Yourself / Carpentry. | HOUSE & HOME / Woodworking. | HOUSE & HOME / Remodeling & Renovation.
Classification: LCC TH2529.W6 W655 2017 | DDC 645/.1--dc23
LC record available at https://lccn.loc.gov/2016049577

Acquiring Editor: Todd R. Berger
Project Manager: Alyssa Bluhm
Art Director: Brad Springer
Layout: Danielle Smith-Boldt

Printed in China

BLACK+DECKER and the BLACK+DECKER logo are trademarks of The Black & Decker Corporation and are used under license. All rights reserved.

**NOTICE TO READERS**

For safety, use caution, care, and good judgment when following the procedures described in this book. The publisher and BLACK+DECKER cannot assume responsibility for any damage to property or injury to persons as a result of misuse of the information provided.

The techniques shown in this book are general techniques for various applications. In some instances, additional techniques not shown in this book may be required. Always follow manufacturers' instructions included with products, since deviating from the directions may void warranties. The projects in this book vary widely as to skill levels required: some may not be appropriate for all do-it-yourselfers, and some may require professional help.

Consult your local building department for information on building permits, codes, and other laws as they apply to your project.

# Contents

## Wood Floors

| | |
|---|---|
| **Introduction** | 7 |
| **Gallery of Wood Flooring Ideas** | 9 |
| **WOOD FLOOR BASICS** | 19 |
| **Planning Your New Wood Floor** | 21 |
| Planning Overview | 22 |
| Floor Anatomy | 23 |
| Floor Selection & Design | 28 |
| **Preparing for a Wood Floor Project** | 37 |
| Floor Covering Removal | 38 |
| Underlayment Removal | 44 |
| Subfloor Repair | 46 |
| Installing Raised Subfloor Panels | 48 |

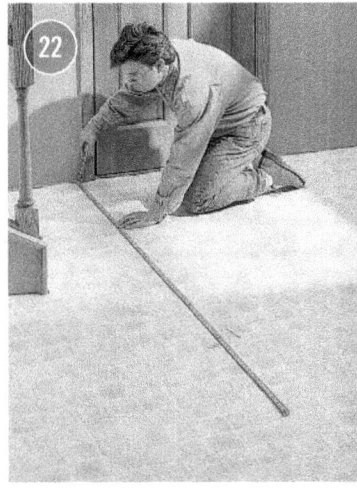

# Contents (continued)

| WOOD FLOOR INSTALLATION | 53 |
|---|---|
| **Installation Techniques** | **55** |
| Transitions for Hardwood Floors | 58 |
| Wood Floor Installation Tips | 62 |
| **Wood Floor Installation** | **65** |
| Strip & Plank Floors | 66 |
| Bonded Bamboo Strip Flooring | 74 |
| Installing Laminate Flooring | 80 |

| **Special Floor Projects** | **91** |
|---|---|
| Parquet Tile | 92 |
| Decorative Medallion | 96 |
| Vintage Wood Floors | 98 |
| End Grain Floors | 104 |
| One-Piece Base Molding | 106 |
| Built-Up Base Molding | 108 |

## FINISH & MAINTAIN WOOD FLOORS — 111

### Finishing Wood Floors — 113
Floor Stains & Finishes — 114
Wax Finishes — 118
Painting Wood Floors — 120

### Maintaining Wood Floors — 125
Cleaning & Maintaining a Wood Floor — 126
Removing Stains from Wood — 128
Refinishing Hardwood Floors — 130
Repairing Scratches & Dents to Hardwood Floors — 140
Fixing Loose & Squeaky Floorboards — 142
Replacing Damaged Floorboards — 144
Replacing a Damaged Stair Tread — 152

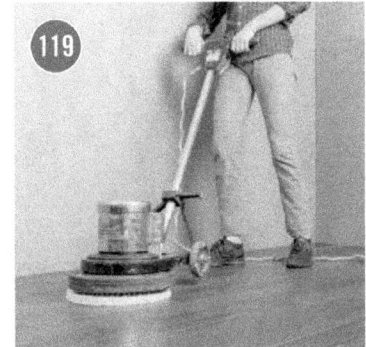

**Resources** — 155
**Photo Credits** — 155
**Metric Conversion Charts** — 156
**Index** — 157

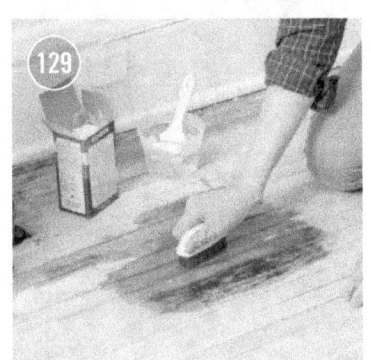

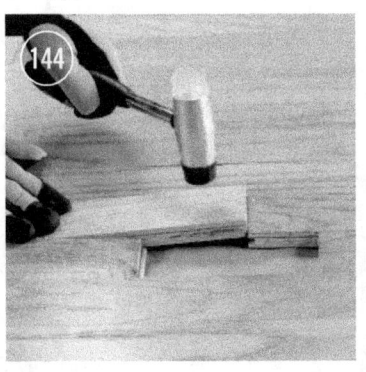

# Introduction

Welcome to the wonderful world of wood flooring. There is nothing quite like the warmth and glow of a pegged plank wood floor. Or the modern sleek lines of lime-washed engineered wood. Or the elegance of the royal parquet. And the best part is, whichever of these you want, you can install yourself!

*BLACK+DECKER Wood Floors* has all the information you need to choose a flooring style, to design, and to measure a new floor, tear out the old floor coverings, install a beautiful new wood floor, and finish and maintain it.

Wood flooring is a fantastic do-it-yourself project because it requires mostly physical labor and attention to detail. Any moderately skilled handy person can do all of the projects in this book.

*BLACK+DECKER Wood Floors* takes you through the process of choosing and installing a wood floor step by step. The book opens with a beautiful gallery of the myriad wood flooring options available. From exotic hardwoods to sustainable bamboo, from medallions and parquets, to repurposed, recycled woods, you can see what all the major manufacturers are offering, what is trending, and what the constant classics are. With the step-by-step photo instructions contained in this book, you will be able to install all these types of floors.

Wood Floor Basics then takes you through all the steps needed to plan and prepare for your wood floor project. Here you can learn how to evaluate your existing floors, how to select and design your new floor, how to measure for materials, and the styles and installation methods of various wood floor products.

Preparing for a Wood Floor Project then gets you into the nitty-gritty of removing existing floor coverings, repairing subfloors, or installing underlayment. If you are thinking of installing wood flooring in your basement, the raised subfloor project gives you the perfect way to keep your new floor dry and mildew free.

Wood Floor Installation is the real meat of the book. The tools you'll need and the techniques needed for success are shown with photos and text. Details like cutting techniques and transitions, and tips for working with stairs and around intrusions are covered. Then, nearly a dozen how-to projects for every kind of wood floor from parquets and end grain tiles to laminates and reclaimed planks is covered with step-by-step directions and detailed photographs.

Wood floors are durable, especially with the new, hardened finishes available today, but they do need maintenance and the occasional repair or refinishing. In Finish & Maintain Wood Floors, the various options for applying original or touch-up finishes are covered, along with a great project for painting floors. Maybe your floor looks good except for a stain or blemish. How-to projects for cleaning, bleaching, or replacing existing boards or planks show you how to remedy the issue. The tips and techniques are presented in full detail.

All in all, *BLACK+DECKER Wood Floors* has got you, and your floors, covered!

# Gallery of Wood Flooring Ideas

The perfect floor is an integral component of any interior design. A well-chosen wood floor will interact with and highlight or downplay other design elements in the room.

The flooring should also be practical and fit the needs of each room. High-traffic areas require woods and finishes that are up to the task. Patterns and colors can hide or amplify wear patterns.

The photos in this section highlight a wide range of wood floor materials, styles, and colors for any room in the home. The following pages are sure to give you new ideas for creative ways to meet your wood floor needs.

**If you want the rich colors** and patterns of exotic tropical wood but want to save the rainforest, laminate is just the ticket. This acacia print looks just like the real thing.

**Random-width engineered maple planks** with a golden stain create an airy, modern feel. This ⅜"-thick, and 3¼"- and 5"-width planks with random length create an upscale look.

**Maple stained a rich auburn** creates a warm, inviting space. A hand-scraped finish makes it appropriate for heavy-traffic areas—it won't show wear like a smooth finish. Finished, hand-scraped maple can be more expensive per square foot.

**Charcoal gray parquet** creates a stunning floor. Parquet floors are available finished or unfinished and in a variety of thicknesses and dozens of wood types.

**Wide planks,** sand-blasted texture, oiled finish, and character galore make these new 11" engineered oak planks appear as though they have been around for centuries.

**Parquet isn't just for European castles.** Parquet is perfect for high-traffic areas because the pattern can mask minor wear and tear.

**An inlayed border on stairs** adds distinctive detail. Available in many patterns, thicknesses, wood types, and finished or unfinished, options with borders abound. Installing an inlayed border is a challenging project for the home DIYer.

**Ten-inch-wide engineered oak planks** with a wire-brushed texture and a factory-applied oil finish complement the Euro feel of this modern laundry room.

**End grain wood tiles** are one of the oldest forms of decorative wood flooring. End grain wood is so durable it was once used to cobble streets.

**Hand-scraped, variable-width engineered planks** add deep color and texture to this airy bedroom. Its ⅜" thickness creates a low profile, perfect for installing over an existing floor, cutting down considerably on project installation time.

**Consider matching your floor to your cabinets.** Bamboo, used here, is eco-friendly, durable flooring available in a wide variety of finishes and widths. Eco-conscious consumers can look for FSC-certified bamboo flooring, often available by special order. Many types of bamboo flooring are less expensive than solid hardwoods.

**Hickory** is a popular wood for wide-plank engineered floors due to its interesting grain pattern. Engineered flooring uses layers of wood to gain the desired thickness. It is often a less-expensive option than solid hardwood. For engineered floors to be stable, don't consider flooring that has thinner than a 3/16" wear layer (the part of the floor you walk on).

GALLERY OF WOOD FLOORING IDEAS

# WOOD FLOOR BASICS

Before starting a big project such as a floor installation, get a handle on the steps necessary for a good outcome.

Understanding how a wood floor is constructed is the first step in creating your own beautiful wood floor. In Planning Your New Wood Floor, you will learn that the first step in a new floor project is to examine the existing flooring. Gaining an understanding of what might need to be repaired, removed, or replaced before a project can begin is crucial. Knowing what you have can play an important role in your upcoming choices.

Floor Selection & Design gives you design tips on all the aspects of floor design. In this section you will learn how the colors, shapes, and sizes of wood floor products affect the overall feel of a room. Durability, ease of installation, and other characteristics are covered so you can feel confident that you are making a good choice. After all, a wood floor can easily last a lifetime, so it's good to have as much information as possible before choosing materials.

Preparing for a Wood Floor Project gets you prepared for the installation of your new floor. The tools you need and the techniques for removing carpet, sheet flooring, tile, and ceramic tile are detailed. In some cases you may need to remove existing underlayment or install new underlayment. You may also find that parts of the subfloor are weakened or damaged and need to be replaced. How-to steps show you exactly how to remove the old and replace with the new. Also included are tips for protecting yourself and your home while you complete the project.

If you have a basement or other area with a concrete slab, directions for how to install a raised subfloor designed for damp areas give you the option of installing wood flooring in these hard to cover areas.

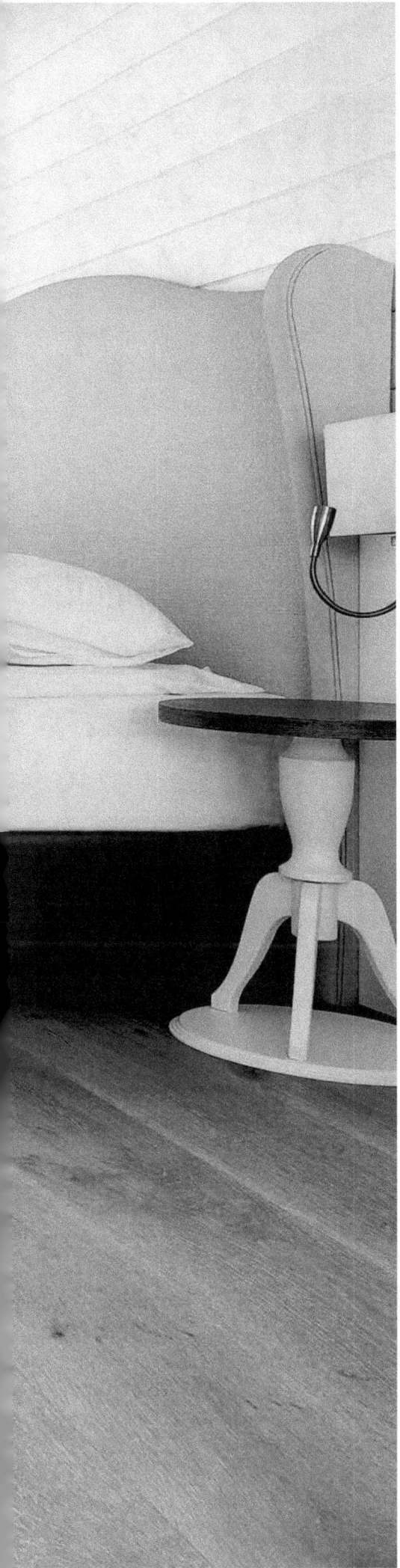

# Planning Your New Wood Floor

Remodeling projects require substantial advance planning. For a wood floor project, it pays to begin with a detailed plan and attention to design. The floor is an integral part of a room, and should be considered with not only the room in mind, but the overall design concept of the house. Wood floors can be exciting attention grabbers or part of the background scenery for other outstanding features. With careful planning, you can create a successful design that flows and integrates with the rest of your design palette.

Keep in mind that hardwood floors and laminates will last a long time. Changing these floor coverings in the future may require removal as the only option. The information in this section will help you understand the anatomy of your existing floor and plan and design new floors to meet your needs.

In this chapter:
- Planning Overview
- Floor Anatomy
- Floor Selection & Design

# Planning Overview

The floor is one of the most visible parts of your decor, which is why appearance is a primary consideration when choosing your new wood floor. Start your search by collecting ideas and inspiration from magazines and books, and visit retail flooring showrooms and home centers to get a sense of what your options are.

As important as appearance is, there are many other considerations that will go into your flooring decision. You'll no doubt put your budget near the top of the list, but you should think about how easy the floor will be to install, how comfortable it is underfoot, its longevity and durability, its resistance to moisture, and how easy it is to clean. You'll also need to assess the demands of the space, including moisture, heavy traffic, and other conditions.

**Measure the area of the project room** to calculate the quantity of materials you'll need. Measure the full width and length of the space to determine the overall square footage, then subtract the areas that will not be covered, such as stairways, cabinets, and other permanent fixtures.

When estimating materials for your project, always add 10 to 15 percent to the total square footage to allow for waste in installation. And always save extra flooring materials just in case you ever need to make a repair.

### CHECKLIST FOR PLANNING A WOOD FLOOR PROJECT

Use this checklist to organize your activities as you start your wood floor project.

- Measure the project area carefully. Be sure to include all nooks and closets, as well as areas under all movable appliances. Calculate the total square footage of the project area.

- Use your measurements to create a floor plan on graph paper.

- If you are installing a medallion, parquet floor, or painting a floor, sketch pattern options on tracing paper laid over the floor plan to help you visualize what the flooring will look like after you install it.

- Identify areas where the type of floor covering will change, and choose the best threshold material to use for the transition.

- Estimate the amount of preparation material needed, including underlayment sheets and floor leveler.

- Estimate the amount of installation material needed, including the floor covering and other supplies, such as adhesive, rosin paper, thresholds, nails or staples, and screws. Add 10 to 15% to your total square footage to allow for waste caused by trimming.

**TIP:** For help in estimating, go to a building supply center and read the labels on materials and adhesives to determine coverage.

- Make a list of the tools needed for the job. Locate sources for the tools you will need to buy or rent.

- Estimate the total cost of the project, including all preparation materials, flooring, installation materials, and tools. For expensive materials, shop around to get the best prices.

- Check with building supply centers or flooring retail stores for delivery costs. A delivery service is often worth the additional charge.

- Determine how much demolition you will need to do, and plan for debris removal through your regular garbage collector or a disposal company.

- Plan for the temporary displacement of furnishings and removable appliances to minimize disruption of your daily routine.

**Cut the carpet** into pieces small enough to be easily removed. If you will be refinishing the underlying hardwood floor, take care not to cut too deeply. Roll up the carpet and remove it from the room, then remove the padding.

**NOTE:** Padding is often stapled to the floor and usually comes up in pieces as you roll it.

## Floor Anatomy

A typical wood-frame floor consists of layers that work together to provide the required structural support and desired appearance. These parts include:

**Joists.** At the bottom of the floor are the joists (or trusses in some homes) 2 × 10 or larger framing members that support the weight of the floor. Joists are typically spaced 16 inches apart on center.

**Subfloor.** The subfloor is nailed to the joists. Most subfloors installed in the 1970s or later are made of ¾-inch tongue-and-groove plywood; in older houses, the subfloor often consists of 1 × 6, 1 × 8, or even 1 × 10 wood planks nailed diagonally across the floor joists.

NOTE: 1× lumber is ¾" thick.

**Underlayment.** On top of the subfloor may be a layer of underlayment. In newer homes, builders place a ½-inch plywood underlayment. If you want to run floorboards in the same direction as the joists, you will need to install underlayment over the subfloor.

**Adhesive.** For some types of wood floors, adhesive is spread on the underlayment before the floor covering is installed.

**Floor covering.** With the exception of some thin profile specialty products, solid hardwood floors are installed with nails or staples. Engineered hardwood floors can be installed with fasteners, with glue, or as a floating floor. Laminate floors typically are floating floors but require adhesive when installed on stairs.

### FLOATING FLOORS

A floating floor doesn't actually float. It is called floating because no adhesives or fasteners are used to attach it to the subfloor. A floating floor usually is installed over an underlayment pad, which may add some sound deadening value.

## Cutaway of a "Before" Floor

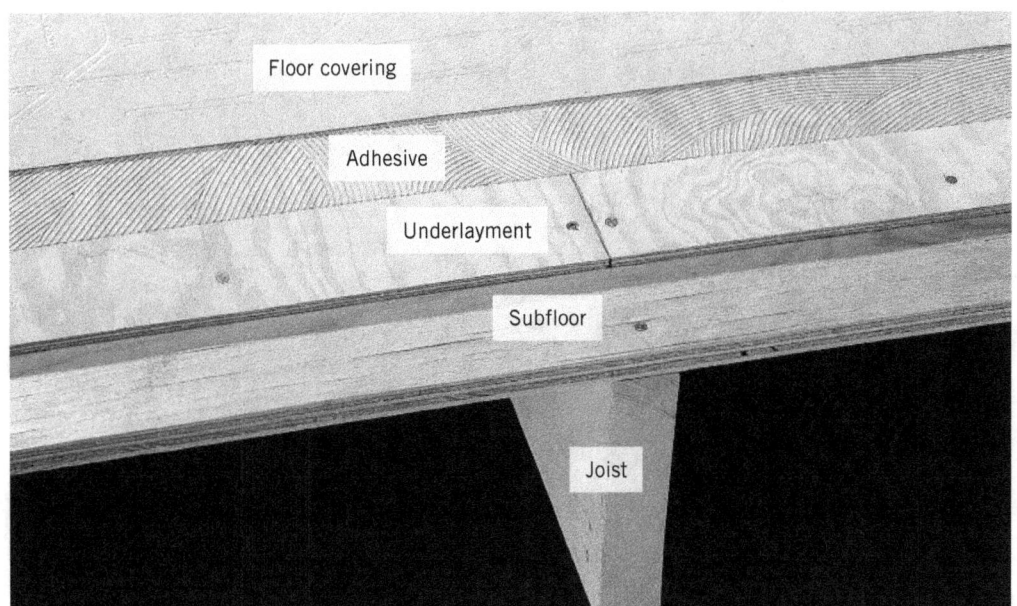

**A modern floor** typically consists of a plywood or oriented strand board subfloor atop 2 × 10 wood joists or engineered trusses. A ¼" or ½" underlayment is installed on top of the subfloor. The floor covering may be glued or nailed to the underlayment.

## Evaluating an Existing Floor

The first step in preparing for rehabbing your old wood floor or installing a new wood floor is evaluating the old floor. Evaluating your floor is a three-step process. Begin by identifying the existing floor material and the installation method used. Is your sheet vinyl attached using the full-spread method or the perimeter-bond method? Is your carpet glued down or stretched? Is the existing hardwood solid or engineered? Next, assess the condition of the floor. Is it securely attached or is it loose in spots? Is it chipped or cracked? Finally, note the height of the existing floor in relation to adjoining floor surfaces. Is it significantly higher than surrounding floors?

Often, a new engineered hardwood or laminate floor can be installed on top of existing flooring. If the existing flooring is not sound or smooth, however, you'll need to do some preparation work. Avoid taking short cuts since this usually results in an inferior final product.

## Evaluating Existing Hardwood Floors

The condition of your floorboards is the primary factor in deciding if refinishing is an option, if the existing floor can serve as a substrate for a new replacement floor, or if a complete tearout is necessary before installing a replacement.

Look for signs of rot, especially around pipes, radiators, and windows. Replacing floorboards is hard work, but possible. Also check for dips or valleys, especially in high-traffic areas. Visually, uneven floors may not seem like a big problem, but they are next-to-impossible to sand because floor sanders do not follow dips and valleys and need to be leveled prior to installation of new material.

If your existing solid wood floor is fairly even and fundamentally sound, you can resurface by sanding or chemically stripping the old finish. For uneven floors, parquet floors, engineered flooring products, and floors that have already been resurfaced, chemically stripping the finish is the better option. Resurface floors only if many scratches, gouges, and stains have affected the floorboards or if you want to stain the floors a different color.

**Older wood floors** may have years of life left. Here an accumulation of wax and dirt is easily removed with mineral spirits, revealing a beautiful floor underneath.

**Identify the type of flooring product.** Standard ¾"-thick hardwood floorboards can withstand one or two resurfacing projects with a drum sander, but some newer flooring products can only be chemically stripped—they simply do not have enough wood to withstand resurfacing. Sanding parquet flooring requires special sanders and is a job for professionals. Otherwise, it should be chemically stripped.

**Look for signs of past resurfacing.** Inexperienced floor refinishers often remove much more wood than is necessary when they power-sand a floor. Look near baseboards and radiators for sanding ridges where the power sander could not reach. If sanding ridges are visible, you probably do not have enough wood remaining above the tongues in tongue-and-groove floorboards to allow you to sand the floors again.

**Grooves begin to splinter** when a tongue-and-groove floor has been sanded too many times. A floor in this condition is a tripping and splinter hazard, but might be suitable underneath new flooring if relatively level.

**Buckling in hardwood floors** usually indicates water damage. The subfloor should be inspected and repaired prior to any new flooring installation. If the subfloor can be inspected from below and is solid, buckled areas may be screwed down and a floating or fastened floor attached if the result is smooth enough.

# Evaluating Other Floor Surfaces

Regardless of which hardwood product you are installing, the manufacturer's instructions are the last word. Carefully read the requirements for your chosen flooring (all are available online) and follow them. Note that there are usually distinctions made for installations using mechanical fasteners versus adhesives. The adhesives necessary will differ based on the application surface. Also note that floor leveling compound might not be an acceptable leveler for mechanically fastened floors.

**High thresholds** often indicate that several layers of flooring have already been installed on top of one another. If you have several layers, it's best to remove them before installing the new wood floor.

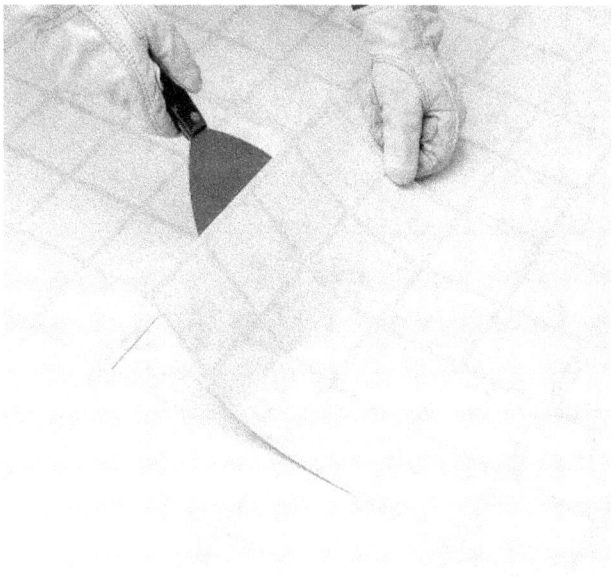

**Loose vinyl or linoleum tiles** may indicate widespread failure of the adhesive. Use a wallboard knife to test tiles. If tiles can be pried up easily in many different areas of the room, plan to remove all of the flooring.

**Air bubbles** trapped under resilient sheet flooring indicate that the adhesive has failed. The old flooring must be removed before the new covering can be installed.

**Cracks in grout joints** around ceramic tile are a sign that movement of the floor covering has caused deterioration of the adhesive layer. If more than 10% of the tiles are loose, remove the old flooring. Evaluate the condition of the underlayment (see page 27) to determine if it also must be removed.

## QUICK GUIDE TO EVALUATING AN EXISTING FLOOR

### RESILIENT FLOORING

**Option 1:** Your existing resilient floor can serve as the foundation for some new wood floor coverings, if the existing surface is relatively smooth and sound. Inspect the existing flooring for loose seams, tears, chips, air bubbles, and other areas where the bond has failed. If these loose spots constitute less than 30% of the total area, you can remove the flooring at these spots and fill the voids with floor-leveling compound. Then, apply embossing leveler to the entire floor and let it dry before laying new flooring.

**Option 2:** If the original resilient flooring is suspect, you can install new underlayment over the old surface after repairing obviously loose areas.

**Option 3:** If the existing surface is in very poor condition, the old resilient flooring should be removed entirely before you install new flooring. If the old flooring was glued down with full-bond adhesive, it's usually easiest to remove both the flooring and underlayment at the same time (page 44). If the old underlayment is removed, you might need to install new underlayment before laying the new wood floor.

### CERAMIC TILE

**Option 1:** If the existing ceramic tile surface is relatively solid, engineered and floating wood floors can sometimes be installed directly over the tile. Inspect tiles and joints for cracks and loose pieces. Remove loose material and fill these areas with a floor-leveling compound.

**Option 2:** If more than 10% of the tiles are loose, remove all of the old flooring before installing the new surface. If the tiles don't easily separate from the underlayment, it's best to remove the tile and the underlayment at the same time, then install new underlayment.

### HARDWOOD FLOORING

**Option 1:** If you're installing a floating floor, you might be able to lay it directly over an existing nailed or glued-down hardwood floor, or you may have to install underlayment. Inspect the flooring and secure any loose areas to the subfloor with spiral-shanked flooring nails or screws, then remove any rotted or buckled wood and fill the voids with plywood of the same height.

**Option 2:** Some engineered or laminate planks require new underlayment over the existing nailed hardwood planks or glued-down hardwood flooring before installation. Run new floorboards in a different direction than current boards by installing them diagonally or perpendicular to the existing floor.

**Option 3:** If the existing floor is a "floating" wood or laminate surface with a foam-pad underlayment, remove it completely before laying any type of new wood or laminate flooring.

### UNDERLAYMENT & SUBFLOOR

Underlayment must be smooth, solid, and level to ensure a long-lasting flooring installation. If the existing underlayment does not meet these standards, remove it and install new underlayment before you lay new flooring.

Before installing new underlayment, inspect the subfloor for chips, open knots, dips, and loose boards. Screw down loose areas, and fill cracks and dips with floor-leveling compound. Remove and replace any water-damaged areas.

### CARPET

Without exception, carpet must be removed before you install any new flooring. For traditional carpet, simply cut the carpet into pieces, then remove the padding and the tackless strips. Remove glued-down cushion-back carpet with a floor scraper using the same techniques as for removing full-bond resilient sheet flooring (see page 41).

### CONCRETE

Moisture content and cleanliness of the concrete are critical factors for hardwood flooring over concrete. Install a proper subfloor, if required by the flooring manufacturer. Engineered wood flooring can typically be installed over concrete at grade level, and some engineered wood and many laminates can be installed below grade level.

**NOTE:** Grade level is the level of the ground surrounding the home. Basements, even walkouts, are considered below grade.

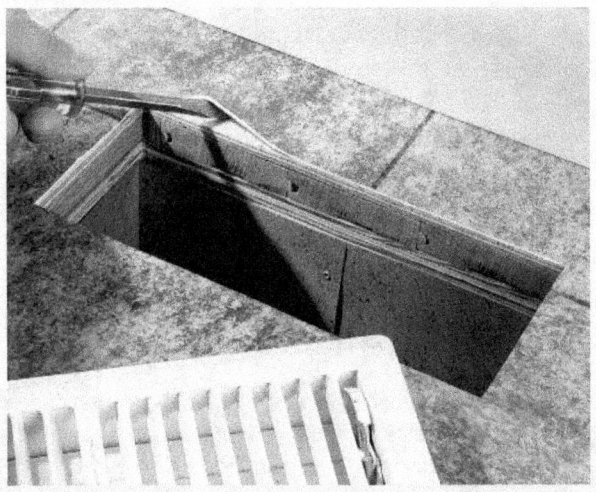

**Determining the number and type of coverings** already on your floor is an important first step in evaluating its condition. Removing this air vent revealed the hardwood tongue-and-groove flooring under the sheet flooring. Unfortunately, installation of the underlayment has probably caused irreparable damage to the hardwood floor.

# Floor Selection & Design

Hardwood flooring is a favorite with homeowners for good reason. The exceptional variety of wood species available means that you can find a look to match just about any decor. The material itself is durable, natural, and extremely long lasting. Wood floors are comfortable underfoot, relatively easy to install, and competitive in price with stone or ceramic tile. Plus, you can choose from a wealth of wood finish colors and patinas for a customized appearance. With the advent of engineered hardwood flooring, the beauty of hardwood floors can be used in even more areas. In this book laminate flooring has been included even though it is not technically wood. Because it is installed in a similar manner, and actually is indistinguishable from wood in many instances, we have chosen to include it here.

**Different tree species** have different grain patterns. Hickory heartwood and sapwood are distinctly different colors.

## Hardwood Flooring

The first concept to understand about hardwood flooring is that it is either solid or engineered. Both are made of wood. Solid wood is simply a board that has been cut into strips or planks and milled with tongues and grooves. Engineered hardwood is a thick layer of veneer glued to a substrate of plywood. It also has tongues and grooves milled into the sides and ends.

Solid wood flooring is usually ¾-inch thick and is installed with nails or staples over a wood subfloor. Some manufacturers produce a ⁵⁄₁₆-inch thin-profile solid wood that can be glued down. Traditionally, solid wood flooring was red or white oak or maple sold in 2¼-inch strips. Now the trend is toward wider planks, up to 6-inches in width and available in many species.

### THE FOREST STEWARDSHIP COUNCIL

The Forest Stewardship Council (FSC) is an international nonprofit group that certifies forests and wood products based on established standards of responsible forest management. Products bearing the FSC stamp have been monitored by third-party officials from the raw material stage in the forest through processing, manufacturing, and distribution as part of their "chain of custody" standards. FSC certification is the best way to ensure that wood products and materials come from sustainable, renewable sources, just like all wood should. For more information, visit www.fsc.org.

Engineered hardwood is usually ⅜-inch thick, but it is available in many other thicknesses, including ¾-inch. The visible veneer layer, which ranges in thickness, is glued to a plywood layer. The wood plies are glued with the grains running perpendicular. This creates a dimensionally stable product. That means that engineered wood does not expand or contract much when exposed to fluctuating temperatures or humidity compared to solid wood. Since its expansion and contraction is limited, engineered hardwood can be installed using glue over any hard surface, including concrete, and can be installed in basements and over in-floor radiant heating. Or, like solid wood, engineered hardwood can be installed with nails or staples.

The price differences between solid and engineered hardwoods may be negligible or substantial. Price differences within the categories might have greater range. Pricing is based on many factors. Solid hardwoods are available in different grades and qualities. The grade of the wood refers to the uniformity of appearance in terms of grain and color and the length of board in addition to the number of defects such as burls, knots, or wormholes.

Quality applies to the number of manufacturing defects such as milling burns or other machining issues. The price differences for engineered hardwoods are based on the thickness of the overall board, the thickness of the veneer, and the quality of the materials used to make the plywood.

### WOOD FLOORING GRADES

Milled wood for flooring is graded by its appearance and average board length. The higher the grade, the less waste occurs during installation due to board length and culling of unsuitable pieces.

**Clear grade** is uniform in color and grain appearance, usually heartwood.

**Select grade** has some variation in color and may include small knots, wormholes, or mineral streaks, a mix of heartwood and sapwood.

**Number 1 Common** can be varied in color and has larger allowable knots than Select.

**Number 2 Common** may have prominent color variation and many character traits like wormholes and knots.

**This maple floor is common #3 grade,** which means numerous variations in color and the inclusion of knots and other character features. While it might not be suitable for a formal dining room, this floor is perfect for a children's play area or den.

**The same species can look very different** with a little staining. This is a maple floor with one board stained to highlight the border pattern. Also notice that the floor field is diagonal.

### SUPER CHEAP SOLID WOOD?

You might see solid wood tongue-and-groove shop grade or odd lots flooring selling for 99 cents a square foot. But it isn't necessarily the deal you think it is. These lots are factory seconds made up of 6"- to 12"-long defective pieces that have been cut out of boards during the inspection process. If you are looking for a highly distressed solid wood floor, this might just be for you, but estimate at least 20% waste when purchasing because some of the pieces will be unusable.

# EXOTIC WOODS

Availability of wood species varies regionally, but most common North American hardwoods are used in the manufacture of flooring. Stock options typically are limited to oak and maple, with cherry, ash, mahogany, walnut, and several other species easily obtained through special order. These North American woods give you plenty of choices for your floor, but even more stunning options are available if you're willing to spend a bit more. Imported exotic species bring with them distinctive and stunning patterns and colors. A sampling includes:

**Ipé. (Brazil)** The Brazilian walnut tree yields boards with grain patterns ranging from regular to very irregular, and an attractive reddish-brown color.

**Wenge. (Africa)** A naturally deep, dark brown—almost black—wood, wenge has long been used for fine wood furnishings. The alluring grain structure appears prominently, and the wood is at its most showy cut in wider planks.

**Patagonian Rosewood. (Chile)** A distinctive option, Rosewood has dark tan colors that lighten over time, and features bold striping throughout the grain that adds an interesting undertone to the natural luster of the wood.

**Cumaru. (Brazil)** A coarse, wavy grain and a reddish tan color that fades over time into an unusual maroon, make this wood an interesting choice. Also called Brazilian Teak.

**Tigerwood. (South America)** A lighter wood, Tigerwood has a unique, extremely irregular, and interlocking grain structure from which it gets its name. The color generally varies from deep golden brown to almost blonde. Tigerwood is best placed in an open, well-lit space, with large uncovered areas showing off the eye-catching grain.

## WOOD HARDNESS SCALE

The Janka scale is used to show the relative hardness, or resistance to impact or wear, of different wood species. In flooring, the benchmark species is northern red oak at 1290, because so many floors are made from this species. The larger the number, the harder the wood. Very hard woods may require drilling pilot holes before driving facenails. Here are some Janka numbers for common and exotic woods used in flooring.

| Ipé | 3680 |
|---|---|
| Brazilian Teak (Cumaru) | 3540 |
| Mesquite | 2345 |
| Hickory | 1820 |
| Wenge | 1620 |
| Hard Maple | 1450 |
| Red Oak | 1290 |
| Walnut | 1010 |
| Southern Pine | 690–870 |

**Ipé scores highest on the Janka hardness scale,** but it is a very dense, tropical wood with a high saturation of natural oil, so it does not stain well. It is used almost exclusively for exterior decks.

## FLOORING THICKNESS

One reason to choose engineered flooring is the finished height of the floor. The ⅜" common thickness of engineered flooring might better match up with existing flooring at transition points. Or, if you are installing flooring over an existing floor, the thinner engineered floor is easier to install under existing fixtures.

# Laminate Flooring

Laminate flooring has become popular in recent years because it is easy to install and relatively inexpensive. Sold in strips or small panels that look like strips, it is constructed of a base layer of wood or paper product to which is bonded a photographic pattern layer that replicates wood floor coverings. It is sold prefinished with a clear, protective wear-layer of highly durable aluminum oxide.

Although some laminate flooring is installed by edge-gluing, nearly all product sold today is put down as a floating floor with click-together joints that have a positive locking action, requiring no fasteners or adhesives (although in many cases, a perimeter bond is recommended). Grain patterns and coloring are available in a nearly infinite number of variations. You can choose a uniform look, making a completed laminate floor unchallenging for the eye or choose a visually intriguing look. Many types of laminates are water resistant, making them good alternatives to solid wood floors in moisture-prone areas, such as below-grade basements and bathrooms.

Laminate flooring is rated by durability using an Abrasion Criteria (AC) rating. The AC rating levels are AC1 through AC5. AC1 through AC3 are designations for residential applications, while AC4 and AC5 are for commercial applications. AC1 floors are recommended for areas such as closets, bedrooms, or guest rooms that receive moderate use. AC2 floors are recommended for general traffic levels, such as living or dining rooms. AC3 products are for heavily trafficked areas such as entryways, kitchens, and playrooms. The commercial products are not recommended for home use as they tend to have a rough surface texture that might be uncomfortable on bare feet. As could be expected, the higher the criteria, the higher the price.

# Design Elements

When considering wood flooring, weigh the same design aspects of any other flooring. Pattern, size of elements, finish, texture, and color are all aspects to consider.

## Pattern

For the most part, wood and laminate flooring have a linear pattern. Using this pattern in different ways can make small rooms look larger and large rooms more cozy. Parquetry is a method of flooring using smaller pieces of wood to create patterns. Parquet flooring can be solid wood laid in a pattern, like herringbone, or wood strips glued onto plywood squares that are installed with adhesive-like tile. Any solid wood or engineered wood strips or planks can be installed in patterns. Parquet tiles are available in everything from the standard four small squares per tile to intricate geometric designs and wavy flowing

**The herringbone pattern** has been around since the beginning of decorative flooring. The pattern can be created with any strip or plank flooring.

patterns. Bold patterns create a focal point and act as exclamation points. Bold floor patterns may limit choices for the rest of the room's design. A big plus for patterns is that they are good at hiding dirt and scratches.

## Size of Elements

Part of the linear pattern is the width of the board. Strip flooring has a width of 3 inches or less. More than 3 inches wide and the board is called a plank. Strip flooring has been the long-standing standard for formal floors and informal floors alike. Wealthy consumers may have chosen other options, but for most homes the strip floor in oak or maple was the most available style during building booms, and therefore the most affordable. Now builders and consumers are much more aware of using flooring as a design element, and manufacturers have responded with hundreds of options. You can find planks up to 12 inches wide. Wide planks used to be only available in pine, but with engineered planks, any species can be used. Wide planks lend an informal yet distinctive look to a room. Many manufacturers also sell planks bundled in varied widths of 3, 5, and 7 inches. The varied widths create another layer of informality.

## Finish

The finish applied to a hardwood floor also affects the feel of a room. With modern urethane finishes, you can choose high gloss or low gloss without worrying about durability. A less shiny, low gloss floor is less likely to show the small scratches that accumulate over the lifetime of a floor. Perhaps the best news in do-it-yourself hardwood flooring is that all styles are now available prefinished. This means you can install your floor and it's done! The greatest value of a factory finish besides no muss and fuss is that these products carry extended wear guarantees. This is possible because the factory finish is applied under controlled settings with techniques like ultraviolet light curing that cannot be duplicated in a home setting.

## Texture

Another aspect of the finish is the texture. Hand-scraped hardwoods and whipsawn planks have incredible individual surfaces. These styles are rustic and add great appeal and a casual feel to any room from the kitchen or den to bedroom. Textures are available on wide planks in most species, but look especially nice with wood species that have prominent grain patterns. Modern looks demand smooth, sleek textures. To achieve a contemporary look, choose woods with fine dense grain patterns like clear maple.

## Color

In combination with texture and element size, color really amps up the design possibilities of wood flooring. The rustic, casual textured floor looks very different when stained a dark mocha versus a whitewashed gray. A smooth floor will also create a different feel with darker or lighter colors. Muted colors won't compete for attention with other design elements in a room. Bold colors will draw attention to the floor itself, and make it much more a component in the overall scheme.

**Prefinished flooring has several advantages over unfinished.** Ease, convenience, and a lack of mess are certainly among them. But it also tends to be more durable and the finish (usually aluminum oxide or lacquer) is smooth and even. On the downside, you are limited in colors and sheens.

# How to Measure Your Room

Before ordering your wood floor, determine the total square footage of your room. To do this, divide the room into a series of squares and rectangles that you can easily measure. Be sure to include all areas that will be covered, such as closets and space under your refrigerator and other movable appliances.

Measure the length and width of each area in inches, then multiply the length times the width. Divide that number by 144 to determine the square footage. Add all of the areas together to figure the square footage for the entire room.

When ordering your flooring, be sure to purchase 10 to 15% extra to allow for waste and cutting. For patterned flooring, you may need as much as 20% extra. Manufacturer's instructions will give additional information on sizing.

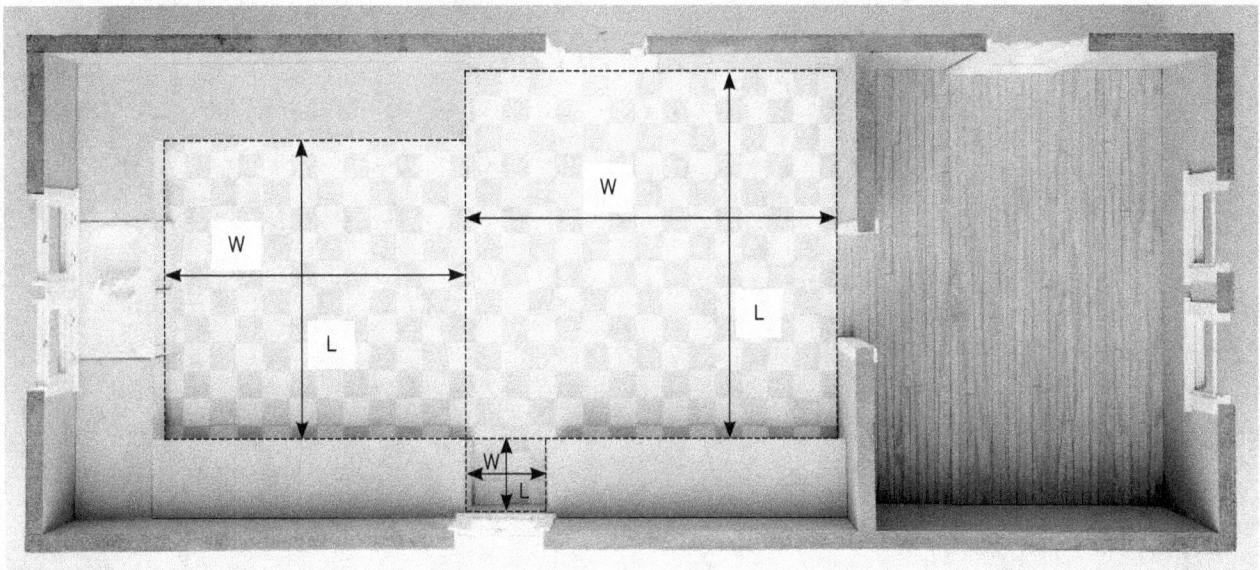

**Divide the room into rectangles or squares.** Include closets and areas where movable appliances are installed. Measure the length and width of each area in inches, then multiply the length times the width. Divide that number by 144 to determine the square footage.

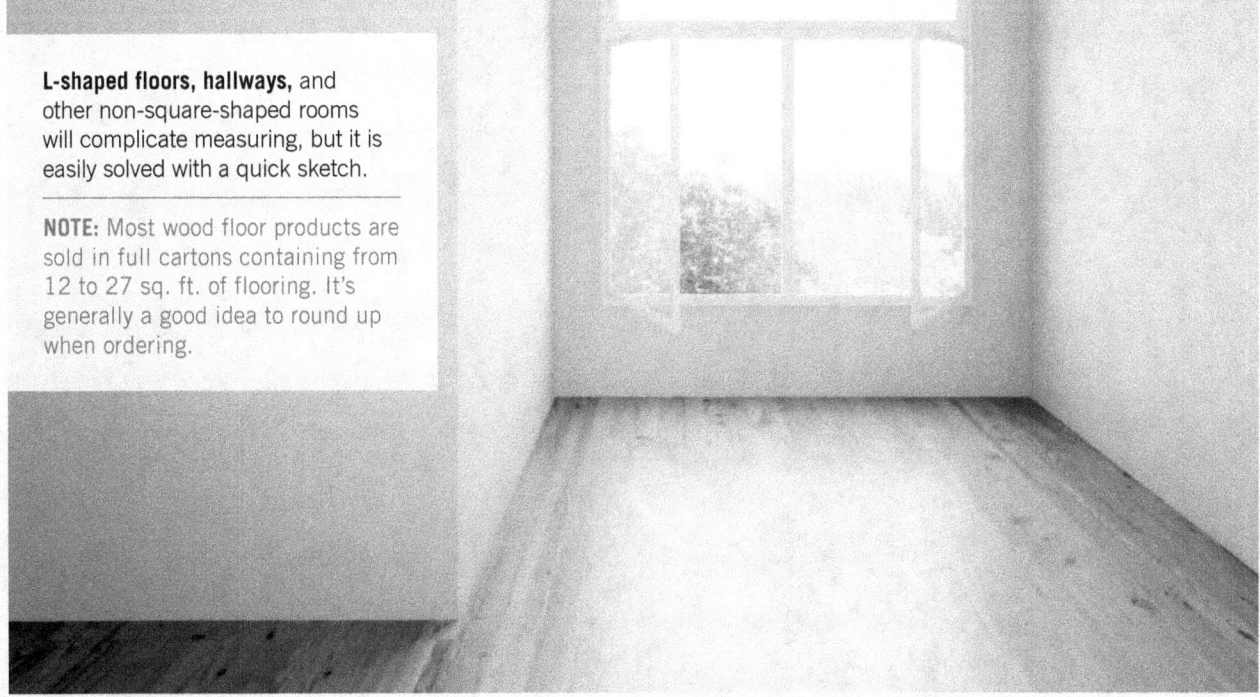

**L-shaped floors, hallways,** and other non-square-shaped rooms will complicate measuring, but it is easily solved with a quick sketch.

**NOTE:** Most wood floor products are sold in full cartons containing from 12 to 27 sq. ft. of flooring. It's generally a good idea to round up when ordering.

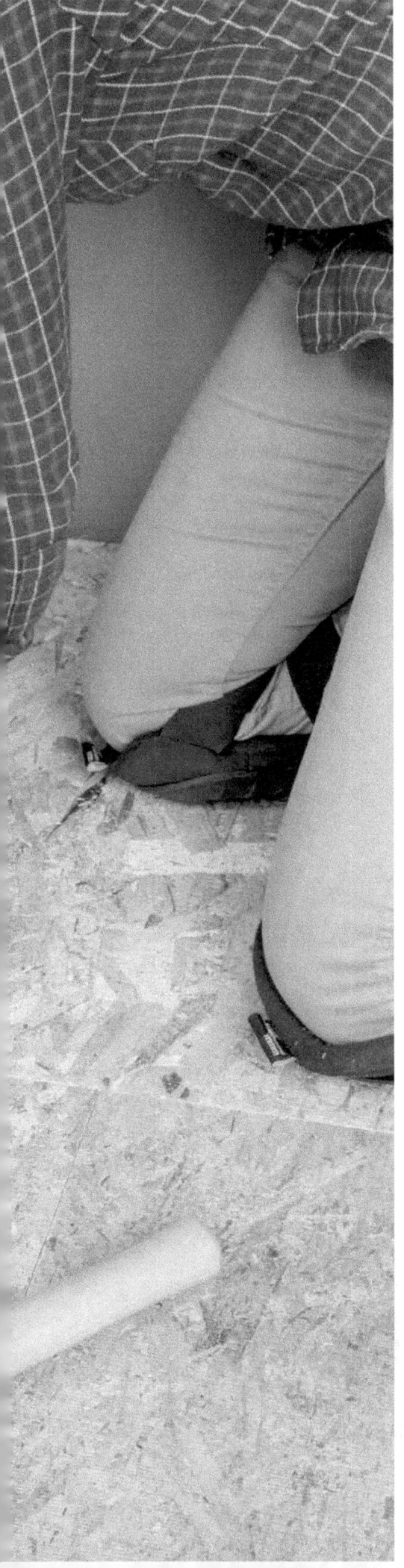

# Preparing for a Wood Floor Project

You have evaluated your existing floors, chosen a design plan, and ordered your hardwood flooring or laminate. Now you are ready to do the preparation to get the space ready for flooring installation.

Before your new floor goes in, your old floor will probably need to be taken out and the subfloor will need to be carefully prepared for a finished surface. Don't assume that imperfections in the subfloor are okay because it will be covered. Some floor finishes may actually accentuate underlying issues. Remember that project preparation is just as important as installing your floor covering and requires the same attention to detail.

Removing old floors, installing new subfloors or underlayments, and filling in cracks and joints isn't the most glamorous job in the world, but it's an investment that will reap big rewards when your flooring project is complete.

If your new floor is part of a larger home improvement project, removing the existing floor should be one of the first steps in the overall project, while installing the new floor is one of the last. All other demolition and construction should be finished in the room before the floor is installed to avoid damaging the new surface.

In this chapter:
- Floor Covering Removal
- Underlayment Removal
- Subfloor Repair
- Installing Raised Subfloor Panels

## Floor Covering Removal

### TOOLS YOU MAY NEED

Floor scraper
Utility knife
Spray bottle
Wallboard knife
Wet/dry vacuum
Heat gun
Hand maul
Masonry chisel
Flat pry bar
Scrap wood
Tape measure
Stapler
Scissors
Eye, ear, and respiratory protection
End-cutting nippers
Liquid dishwashing detergent
Belt sander (optional)
Sheet plastic
Masking tape
Screwdriver
Box fan
Work gloves

When old floor coverings must be removed, as is the case with many projects, thorough and careful removal work is essential to the quality of the new flooring installation.

The difficulty of flooring removal depends on the type of floor covering and the method that was used to install it. Carpet and perimeter-bond vinyl are generally very easy to remove, and removing vinyl tiles is also relatively simple. Full-spread sheet vinyl can be difficult to remove, however, and removing ceramic tile can be a lot of work.

With any removal project, be sure to keep your tool blades sharp, and take care not to damage the underlayment if you plan to reuse it. If you'll be replacing the underlayment, it may be easier to remove the old underlayment along with the floor covering.

Use a floor scraper to remove resilient floor coverings and to scrape off leftover adhesives or backings. The long handle provides leverage and force, and it allows you to work in a comfortable standing position. A scraper will remove most of the flooring, but you may need other tools to finish the job.

## Dust and Debris Containment

**Cover entryways** with sheet plastic to contain dust and debris while you remove the old floor.

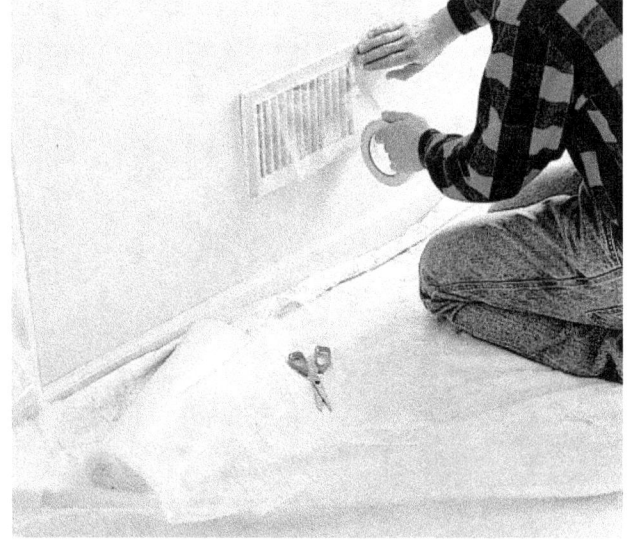

**Cover heat and air vents** with sheet plastic and masking tape to prevent dust and debris from entering ductwork.

### ASBESTOS AND FLOORING

Resilient flooring manufactured before 1980 may contain asbestos, which can cause severe lung problems if inhaled. The easiest method for dealing with asbestos-containing flooring is to cover it with a new floor covering. If the asbestos flooring must be removed, consult an asbestos-abatement professional or ask a local building inspector to explain the asbestos handling and disposal regulations in your area.

## Tools for Floor Covering Removal

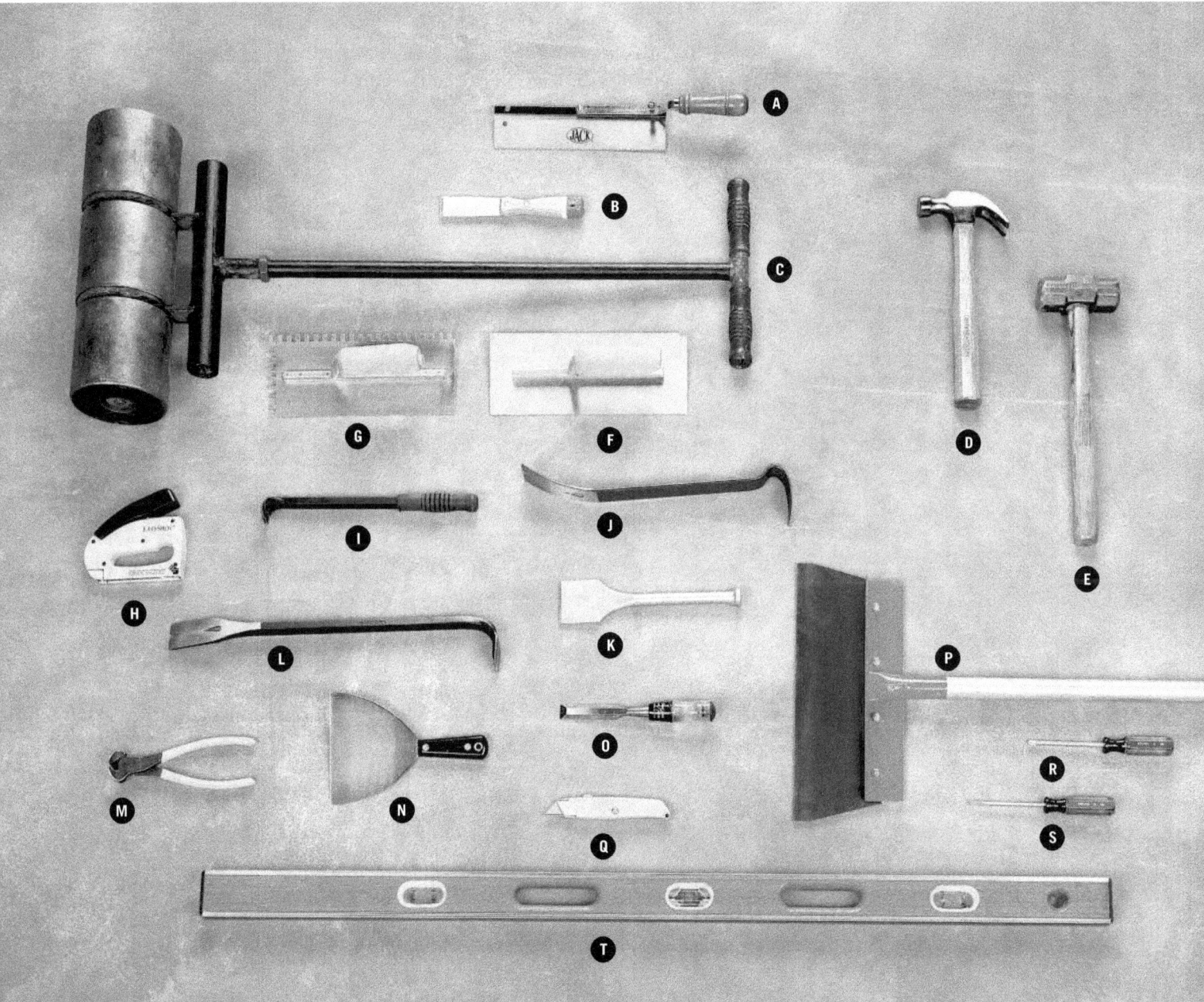

**Hand tools for flooring removal and surface preparation include:** jamb saw (A), putty knife (B), floor roller (C), hammer (D), hand maul (E), flat-edged trowel (F), notched trowel (G), stapler (H), cat's paw (I), flat pry bar (J), masonry chisel (K), crowbar (L), nippers (M), wallboard knife (N), wood chisel (O), long-handled floor scraper (P), utility knife (Q), Phillips screwdriver (R), standard screwdriver (S), and carpenter's level (T).

How to Remove Baseboards

**Cut the paint** away from the baseboard with a utility knife.

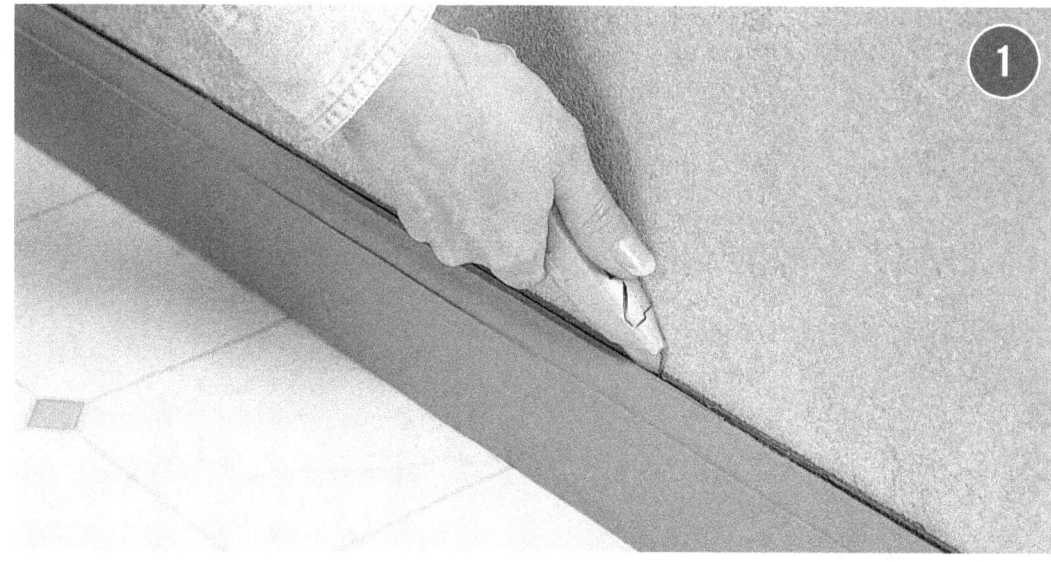

**Remove the baseboard** using a pry bar placed against a scrap board. Pry the baseboard at all nail locations. Number the baseboards as they are removed.

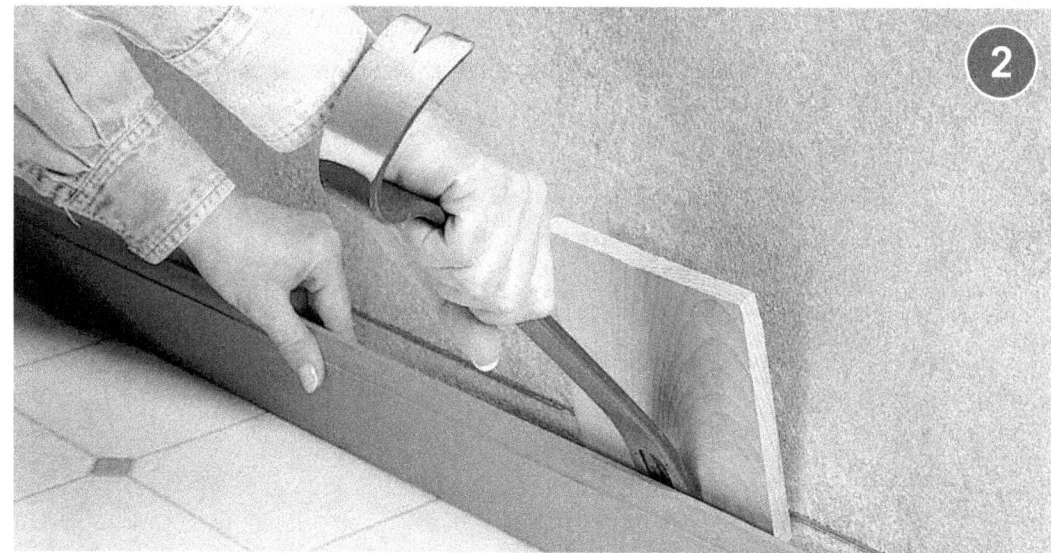

**Remove the nails** by pulling them through the back of the baseboard with nippers or pliers.

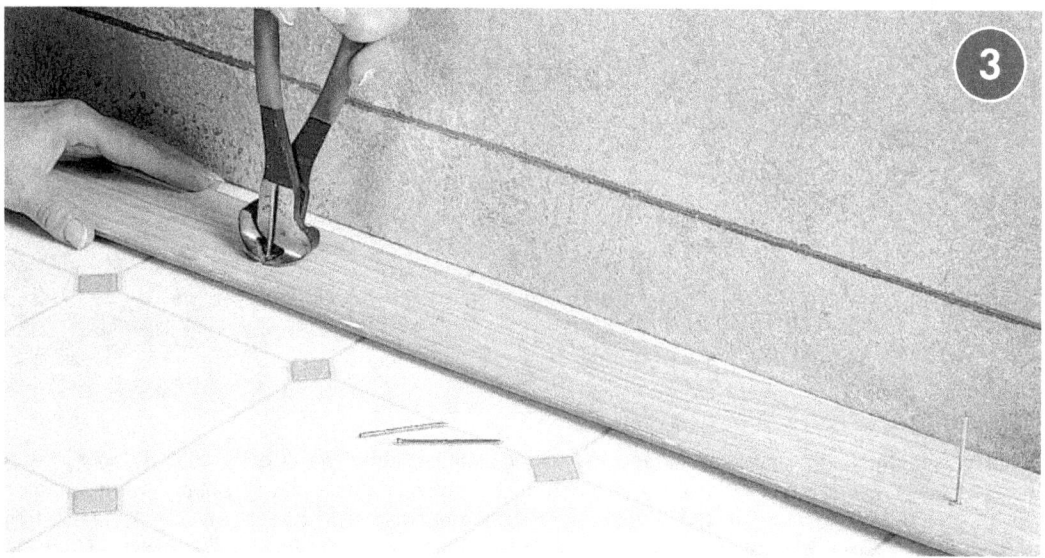

# How to Remove Sheet Flooring

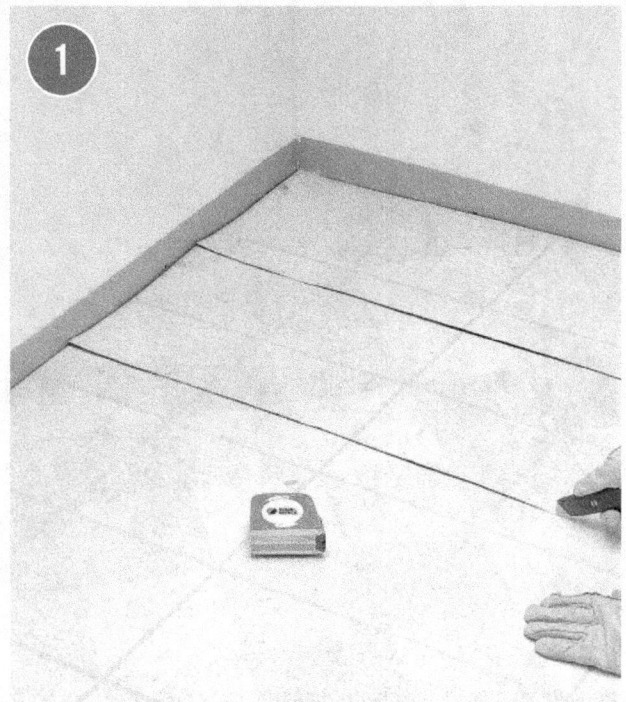

**Use a utility knife** to cut the old flooring into strips about a foot wide to make removal easier.

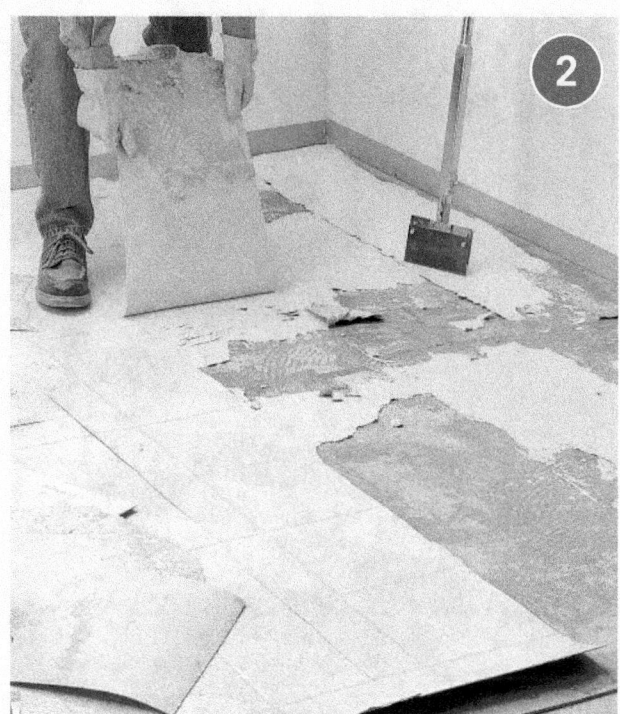

**Pull up as much flooring as possible by hand.** Grip the strips close to the floor to minimize tearing.

**Cut stubborn sheet vinyl** into strips about 6" wide. Starting at a wall, peel up as much of the floor covering as possible. If the felt backing remains, spray a solution of water and liquid dishwashing detergent under the surface layer to help separate the backing. Use a wallboard knife to scrape up particularly stubborn patches.

**Scrape up the remaining sheet vinyl** and backing with a floor scraper. If necessary, spray the backing with the soap solution to loosen it. Sweep up the debris, then finish the cleanup using a wet/dry vacuum.

**TIP:** Add about an inch of water to the vacuum container to help control dust.

## How to Remove Resilient Tile

**Starting at a loose seam,** use a long-handled floor scraper to remove tiles. To remove stubborn tiles, soften the adhesive with a heat gun, then use a wallboard knife to pry up the tile and scrape off the underlying adhesive.

**Remove stubborn adhesive or backing** by wetting the floor with a mixture of water and liquid dishwashing detergent, then scrape it with a floor scraper.

## How to Remove Ceramic Floor Tile

**Knock out tile** using a hand maul and masonry chisel. If possible, start in a space between tiles where the grout has loosened. Be careful when working around fragile fixtures, such as drain flanges, to prevent damage.

**If you plan to reuse the underlayment,** use a long-handled floor scraper to remove any remaining adhesive. You may have to use a belt sander with a coarse sanding belt to grind off stubborn adhesive.

# How to Remove Carpet

**Use a utility knife** to cut around metal threshold strips to free the carpet. Remove the threshold strips with a flat pry bar.

**Cut the carpet** into pieces small enough to be easily removed. If you will be refinishing the underlying hardwood floor, take care not to cut too deeply. Roll up the carpet and remove it from the room, then remove the padding.

**NOTE:** Padding is often stapled to the floor and usually comes up in pieces as you roll it.

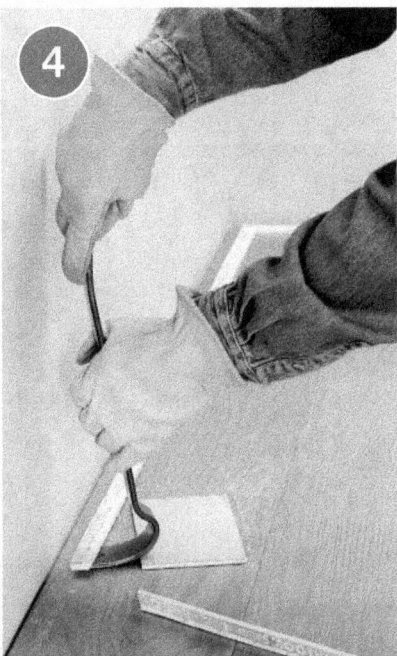

**VARIATION:** To remove glued-down carpet, cut it into strips with a utility knife, then pull up as much material as you can. Scrape up the remaining cushion material and adhesive with a floor scraper.

**Use end-cutting nippers or pliers** to remove all of the staples from the floor. Run your bare hand over the surface to find any partial staples that might not be visible.

**Remove tackless strips immediately** from the perimeter of the room. Pry them loose with a pry bar. Always wear gloves when handling tackless strips.

PREPARING FOR A WOOD FLOOR PROJECT • 43

# Underlayment Removal

Flooring contractors routinely remove the underlayment along with the floor covering before installing new flooring. This saves time and makes it possible to install new underlayment that's ideally suited to the new flooring. Do-it-yourselfers using this technique should make sure to cut the flooring into pieces that can be easily handled.

### WARNING

This floor removal method releases flooring particles into the air. Be sure the flooring you are removing does not contain asbestos. See Asbestos & Flooring, page 39.

### TOOLS & MATERIALS

Gloves
Circular saw with carbide-tipped blade
Flat pry bar
Mallet
Reciprocating saw
Wood chisel
Hammer
Dust mask
Eye and ear protection
Work gloves

### REMOVAL TIP

**Examine fasteners** to see how the underlayment is attached. Use a screwdriver to expose the heads of the fasteners. If the underlayment has been screwed down, you'll need to remove the floor covering and then unscrew the underlayment. If the underlayment has been nailed, you can pry it up without separating the floor covering.

**Remove the underlayment and floor covering** as though they're a single layer. This is an effective removal strategy with any floor covering that's bonded to the underlayment.

## How to Remove Underlayment

**Adjust the cutting depth of a circular saw** to equal the combined thickness of your floor covering and underlayment. Using a carbide-tipped blade, cut the floor covering and underlayment into squares measuring about 3' square. Be sure to wear safety goggles and gloves.

**Use a reciprocating saw to extend the cuts** to the edges of the walls. Hold the blade at a slight angle to the floor and be careful not to damage walls or cabinets. Don't cut deeper than the underlayment. Use a wood chisel to complete cuts near cabinets.

**Separate the underlayment from the subfloor** using a flat pry bar and hammer. Remove and discard the sections of underlayment and floor covering immediately, watching for exposed nails. If underlayment is attached to the subfloor with screws, see Tip, page 44.

**VARIATION:** If your existing floor is ceramic tile over plywood underlayment, use a hand maul and masonry chisel to chip away the tile along the cutting lines before making cuts. Protect your saw guard with masking tape and use a cement cutting blade. Using a vacuum attached to the dust port will help moderate the dust created by this method.

# Subfloor Repair

A solid, securely fastened subfloor minimizes floor movement and squeaks. It also prevents deflection, or vertical movement, which is detrimental to most wood floor installations.

After removing the old underlayment, inspect the subfloor for loose fasteners, moisture damage, cracks, and other flaws. If your subfloor is made of dimension lumber rather than plywood, you can use plywood to patch damaged sections. If the plywood patch doesn't reach the height of the subfloor, add layers of thinner material or use floor leveler or building paper to raise the surface so it is even with the surrounding area.

Floor leveler is used to fill in dips and low spots in plywood subfloors. Mix the leveler according to directions from the manufacturer, adding a latex or acrylic bonding agent for added flexibility, if specified.

### TOOLS & MATERIALS

| | |
|---|---|
| Flat-edged trowel | Tape measure |
| Drywall knife | Deck screws (1", 2") |
| Straightedge | Carpenter's level |
| Framing square | Plywood or underlayment |
| Drill | 2 × 4 lumber |
| Circular saw | 10d common nails |
| Cat's paw | Power sander |
| Wood chisel | Floor patching compound |
| Hammer | Protective gloves |
| Floor leveler | Eye and ear protection |

Always check the specification on both subfloors and underlayment for your chosen wood floor. Some wood floors only require a subfloor, but others require subfloor and underlayment. A successful wood floor installation depends on the proper structure underneath.

## How to Replace a Section of Subfloor

**Use a framing square** to mark a rectangle around the damage, making sure two sides of the rectangle are centered over floor joists. Remove nails along the lines using a cat's paw. Make the cuts using a circular saw adjusted so the blade cuts through the subfloor only. Use a jigsaw or a chisel to complete cuts.

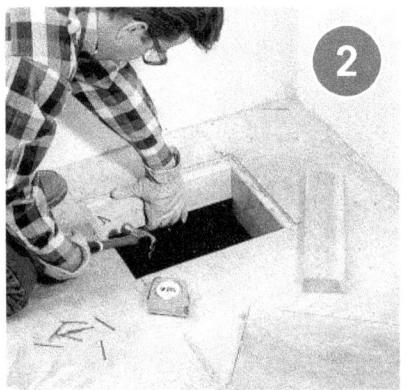

**Remove the damaged section,** then nail two 2 × 4 blocks between the joists, centered under the cut edges for added support. If possible, nail the blocks from below. Otherwise, toenail them from above using 10d nails.

**Measure the cut-out section,** then cut a patch to fit. Use material that's the same thickness as the original subfloor. Fasten the patch to the joists and blocks using 2" deck screws spaced about 5" apart.

## How to Apply Floor Leveler

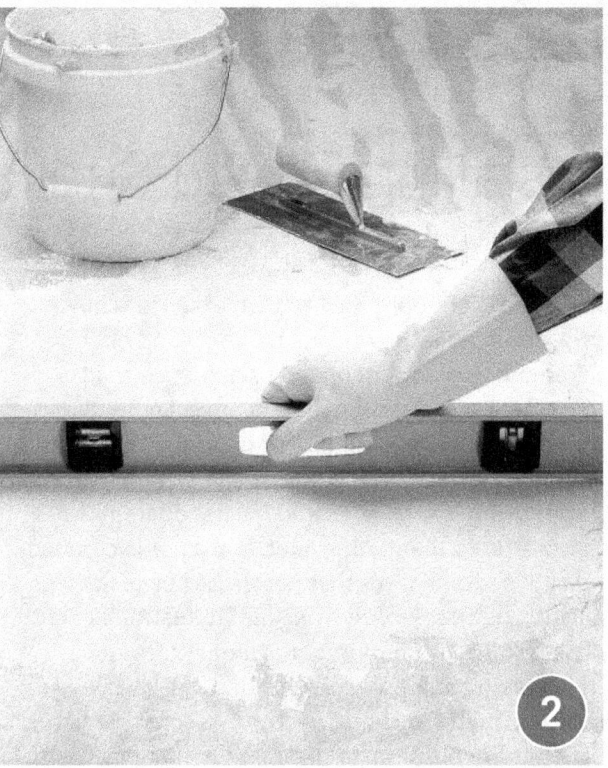

**Mix the leveler according to the manufacturer's directions,** then spread it onto the subfloor using a trowel. Build up the leveler in thin layers to avoid overfilling the area, allowing each layer to dry before applying the next.

**Use a straightedge** to make sure the filled area is level with the surrounding area. If necessary, apply more leveler. Allow the leveler to dry, then shave off any ridges with the edge of a trowel, or sand it smooth.

## How to Install Plywood Underlayment

**Continue fastening sheets of plywood** to the subfloor, driving the screw heads slightly below the underlayment surface. Leave ¼" expansion gaps at the walls and between sheets. Offset seams in subsequent rows.

**Install a piece of plywood underlayment** along the longest wall, making sure the underlayment seams are not aligned with the subfloor seams. Fasten the plywood to the subfloor using 1" deck screws driven every 6" along the edges and at 8" intervals in the field of the sheet.

**Mix floor-patching compound** and latex or acrylic additive following the manufacturer's directions. Spread it over seams and screw heads using a drywall knife.

# Installing Raised Subfloor Panels

Raised subfloor panels are an excellent choice as a base layer when installing wood or laminate floors over concrete slabs, such as in a basement. The raised panels do an even better job of protecting against moisture than simple plastic vapor barriers. Raised panels are designed with three layers: a surface layer of wood wafer board or MDF, a waterproof membrane later, and a honeycombed plastic pedestal layer that raises the entire flooring slightly off the slab, allowing air circulation beneath. The result is a subfloor that is largely immune to the nagging mildew problems that can plague flooring materials laid directly on a concrete slab in a basement. As an added benefit, the panels also increase the insulation value of the floor, making a basement considerably cozier. In fact, a variation is available that increases the R-value of the floor even more.

Do not expect a raised subfloor to eliminate problems in a basement with severe water problems, however. The system works very well for combatting the normal moisture that is always present in an otherwise water-secure basement, but a basement that frequently has puddled water must be corrected in a more aggressive way before flooring can be laid over the slab.

The raised subfloor panels fit together securely with simple tongue-and-groove edges, and for best results the concrete slab must first be examined for dips or cracks, and leveled out before laying the subfloor panels.

### TOOLS & MATERIALS

| | |
|---|---|
| Long board | Leveling shims |
| Floor leveler and trowel (if needed) | Tapping block and pull bar |
| Tape measure | Hammer |
| Circular saw | ¼" wall spacers |
| Jigsaw | Particle mask |
| Carpenter's square | Eye and ear protection |
| | Work gloves |

**A raised subfloor system for a laminate floor in cross section:** three-ply DRIcore panel (A) including raised pedestal layer, waterproofing layer, and wood waferboard layer; foam underlayment (B); subloor (C); laminate flooring (D).

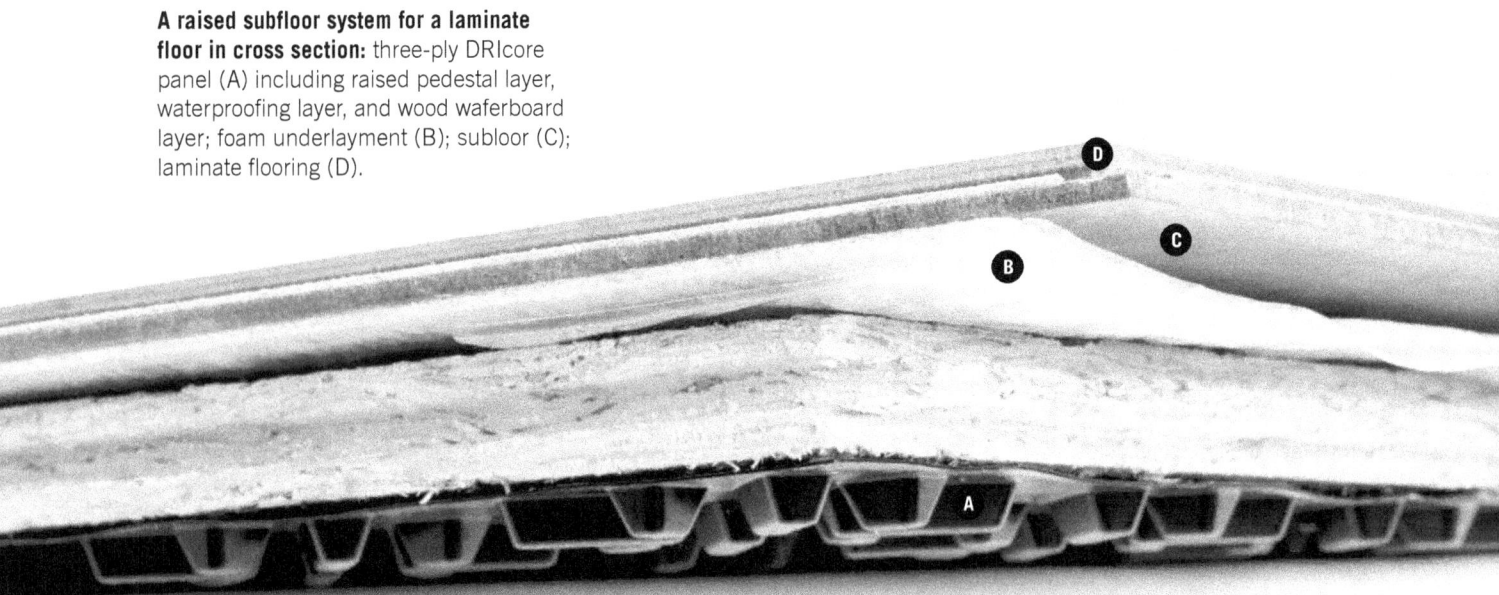

# How to Install Raised Subfloor Panels over a Concrete Slab

**OPTION:** Following the manufacturer's instructions, mix the floor leveler with water. The batch should be large enough to cover the entire floor area to the desired thickness (up to 1"). Pour the leveler over the floor.

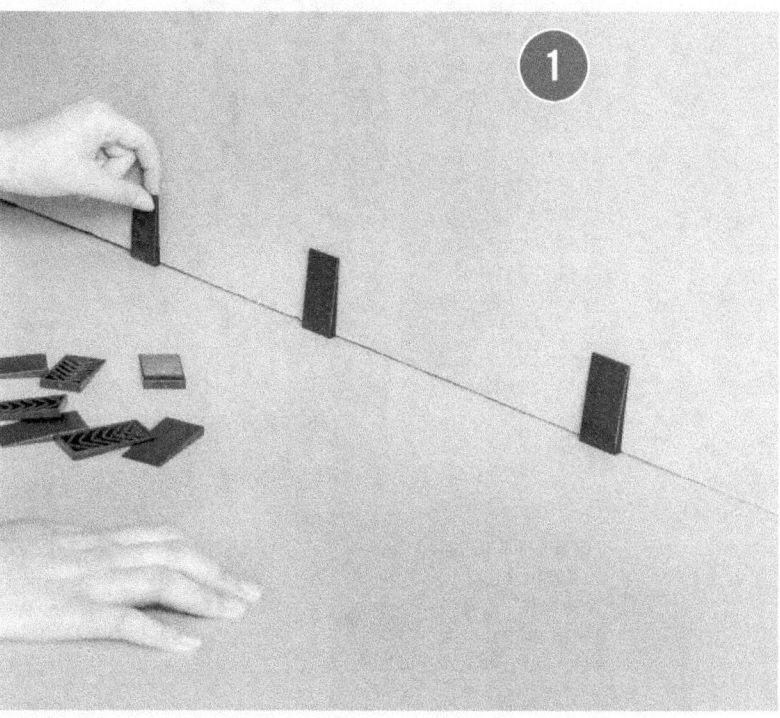

**Clean the concrete floor** and install temporary ¼" spacers along all walls.

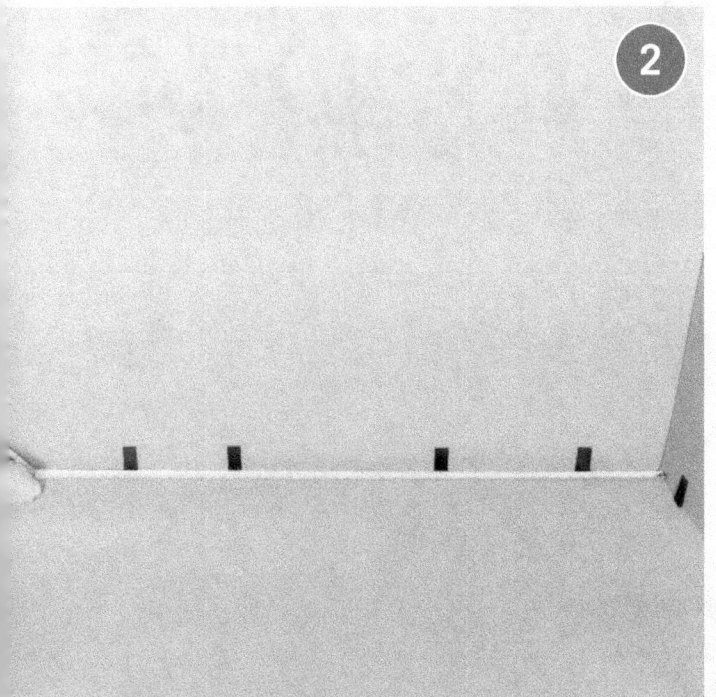

**Starting with the longest wall,** measure the length of the wall, and calculate the number of panels needed by dividing this length by the width of the panel (most products are 2 × 2'). If necessary, trim the starting panel to ensure that the last panel in the first row will be at least 3" in width.

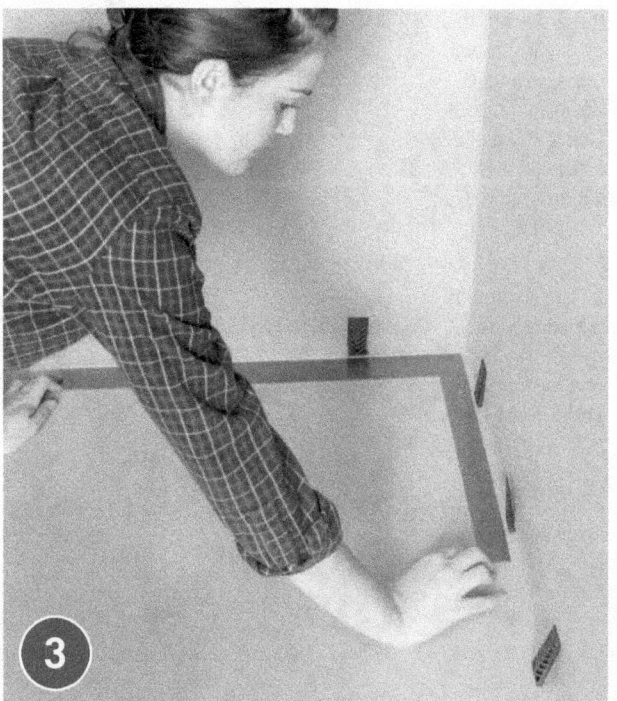

**Check the first corner for square,** using a carpenter's square. If it is not square, the first panel will need to be angled in the back corner to ensure the first row will fit flush against the wall along its entire length.

*(continued)*

PREPARING FOR A WOOD FLOOR PROJECT • 49

**Lay the first panel with the tongue side flat against the wall spacers.** Slide the next panel into place by connecting its tongue into the groove of the preceding panel. Using a tapping block, snug up the tongue-and-groove joint.

**For the last panel in the first row,** measure the gap between the last installed panel and the wall spacer, and cut the last panel to this measurement. Install by inserting the tongue of the cut panel into the groove of the preceding panel, and levering it down into place. Pull it into place so the joint is secure using a pull bar.

**Before beginning the second row,** check the first row for flatness, and if there are any areas with "give" or bounce, adjust them with leveling shims inserted under the panels.

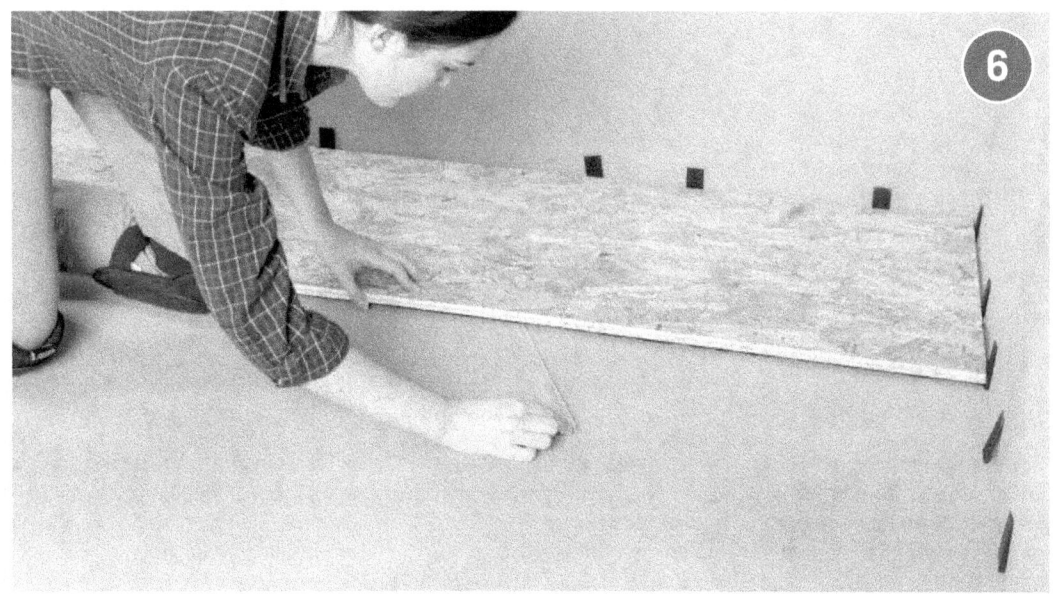

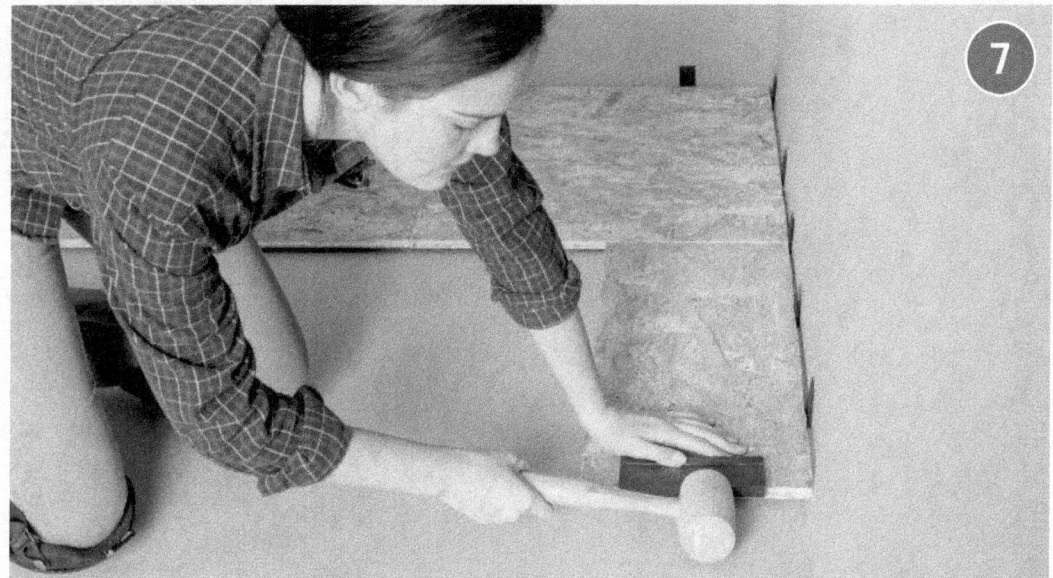

**As you start the second row,** cut the first panel in half, so that seams will be staggered between rows. Begin with the half panel, and install the second row as you did the first, sliding the tongues into the grooves of the preceding row, and snugging them up with the tapping block.

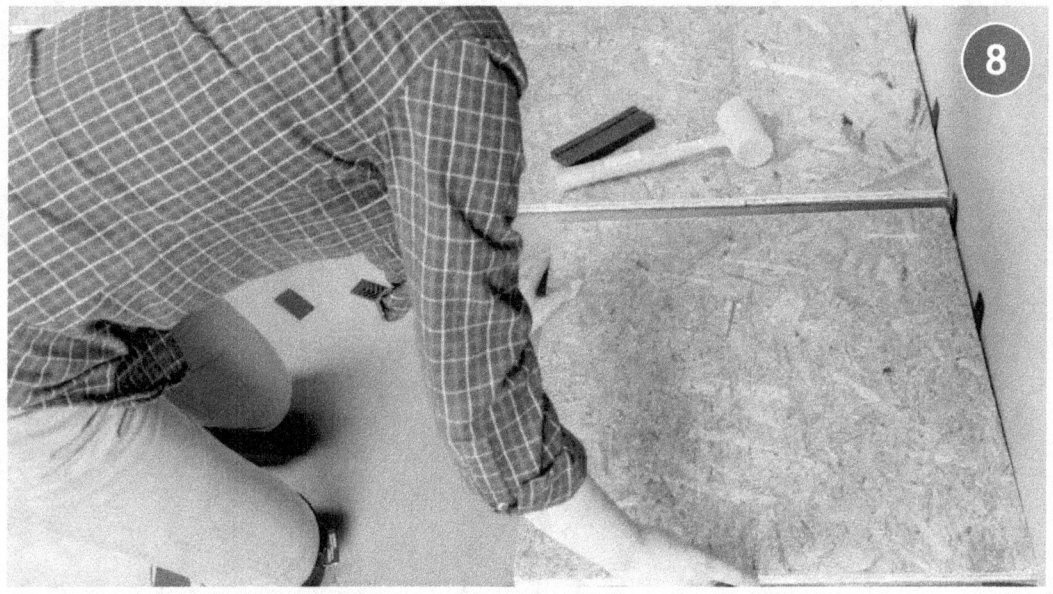

**Install the subsequent rows,** so that the first panels alternate, with odd number rows matching the pattern of the first row, even numbered rows matching the pattern of the second row.

**At the last row,** trim the wall side of the panels to fit the space between the previous row and the wall spacers, and snug up their joints with the pull bar. Remove all spacers.

**Spread flooring strips or planks** out in the installation area and let them acclimate for a day before installation.

# WOOD FLOOR INSTALLATION

How you install a wood floor depends, of course, on the materials you are using. Some wood floors may be nailed or stapled in place, glued in place, or locked in place with engineered pieces that click together. Whatever the installation technique, many common aspects apply to almost every wood floor.

Installation Techniques introduces the tools you need to complete any of the installation projects that follow. Though many flooring tools are common to any carpentry job, there are a few specialty tools that make completing your project easier. These are clearly identified so you can easily find or rent them.

Very few rooms exist as simply a square box perfectly sized to flooring materials, so knowing how to cut various types of wood flooring is critical. Also important is how to deal with protrusions into the installation area—such as fireplace aprons, doorways, radiators and vents, and thresholds. Your floor will probably transition to another room with a different floor, so creating an attractive connection is important. In some cases you may have moved or removed a wall or door and now have to patch the area. A number of options for accomplishing this are shown.

The four wood flooring installation projects presented here cover most of the types of hardwood installations. Here you will find complete step-by-step photo how-to instructions for installing a hardwood plank floor with nails or staples, a fully bonded wood strip floor, and a bamboo strip floor. The so-called floating floors, because they are not fully attached to the subsurface, are also covered in detail.

Special Floor Projects has a number of projects designed to give you a truly unique floor. How to install parquet tiles, decorative medallions, and end grain flooring is covered. In addition, how to use salvaged lumber and salvaged flooring to create a distinctive old new floor is presented. You can learn how to make your own tongue-and-groove flooring from reclaimed planks, tips for reusing salvaged floorboards, and how to create a one-of-a-kind end grain floor.

Finally, remember that flooring manufacturers have created specific installation directions for all of their products. Regardless of what you read here, those installation directions are your number one source of information for your specific product. Make certain that you read their recommendations on fasteners or adhesives and subfloor or underlayment requirements. Remember, a well-installed modern wood floor can last a lifetime. Take the time to install it properly.

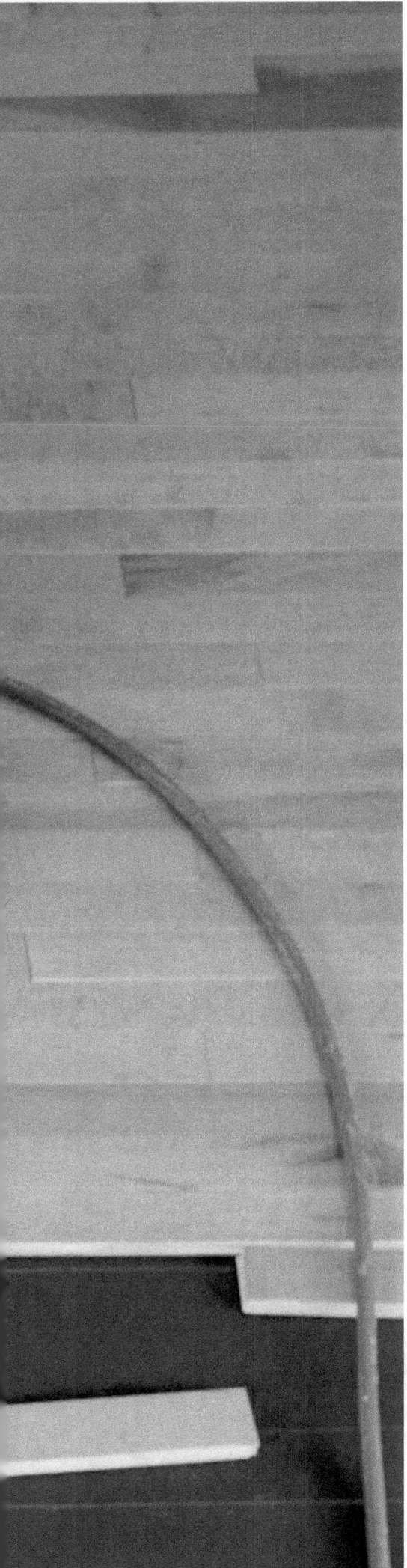

# Installation Techniques

Using the proper techniques helps you create the most beautiful floor.

All wood flooring must be acclimated to the space before it is installed. This allows the flooring to come to the same moisture content as the subfloor and surrounding structures. Because wood expands and contracts with temperature and humidity, the flooring being installed must be at the same level as the surrounding materials or problems will arise.

Flooring is always installed with a gap between it and the surrounding walls (except on staircases). The gap is then covered with base molding. The gap is necessary due to the expansion and contraction of the walls and floors. To maintain even gaps it is helpful to create a number of ⅜- to ½-inch-thick shims to place along the walls prior to installation or drive a row of nails ⅜ to ½ inch from the walls.

When laying out strip, plank, or laminate flooring, loosely dry fit a run of flooring 2 or 3 feet wide. Offset board ends by at least 6 inches (preferably more). If using solid wood, check each piece for splits or bark inclusions. Cut out the imperfections and use these shorter pieces around the room edges.

Whether you are installing by nailing or gluing, all wood flooring relies on a tongue-and-groove system to stabilize the joints between each piece. In some instances you will need to cut tongues or grooves off, join two grooved sides with a spline, or use glue to stabilize a transition that does not have tongue or groove.

In this chapter:
- Transitions for Hardwood Floors
- Wood Floor Installation Tips

# Cutting Hardwood Floors

**Rip-cut hardwood planks from the back side** to avoid splintering the top surface. Measure the distance from the wall to the edge of the last board installed, subtracting ½" to allow for an expansion gap. Transfer the measurement to the back of the flooring, and mark the cut with a chalk line.

**When rip-cutting hardwood flooring with a circular saw,** place another piece of flooring next to the one marked for cutting to provide a stable surface for the foot of the saw. Clamp a cutting guide to the planks to ensure a straight cut.

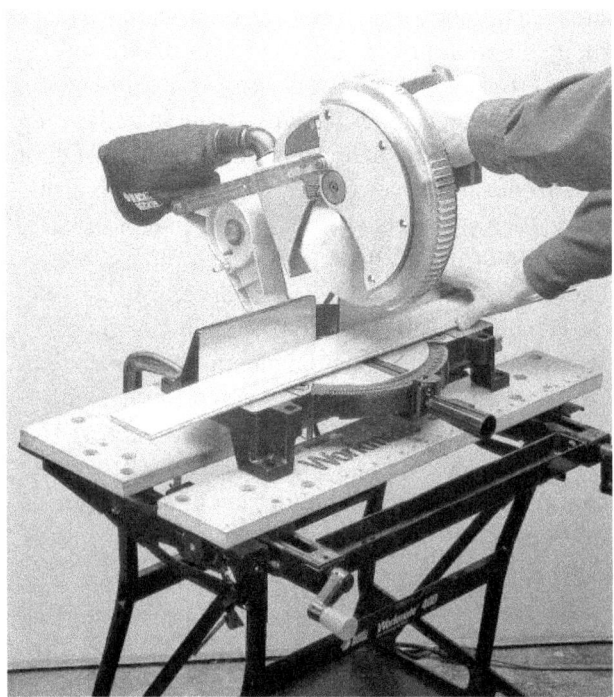

**Crosscut hardwood flooring using a power miter saw.** Place the top surface face up to prevent splintering.

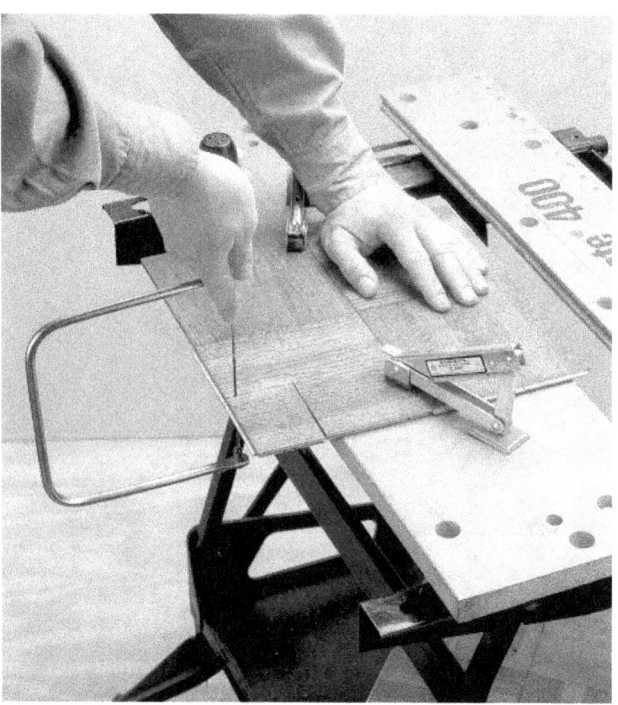

**Make notched or curved cuts in hardwood flooring** with a coping saw or jigsaw. If using a jigsaw, the finished surface should face down. Clamp the flooring to your work surface when cutting.

# Tools for Installing Hardwood Floors

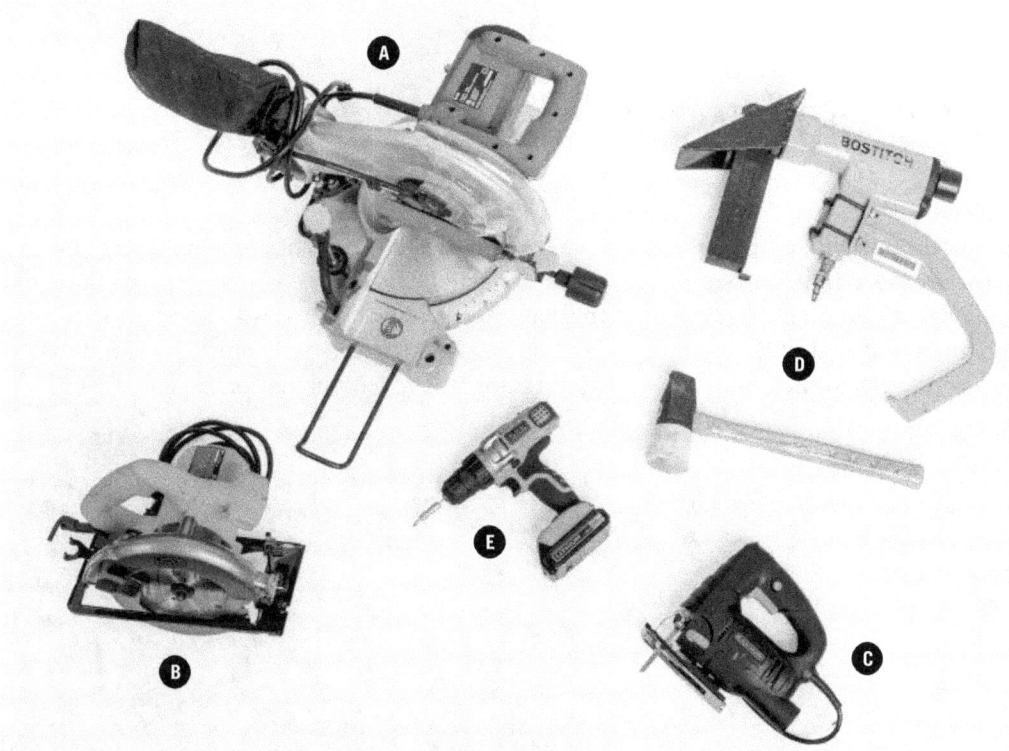

**Power tools for hardwood flooring installation include:** miter saw (A), circular saw (B), jigsaw (C), pneumatic flooring nailer and flooring hammer (D), cordless drill (E).

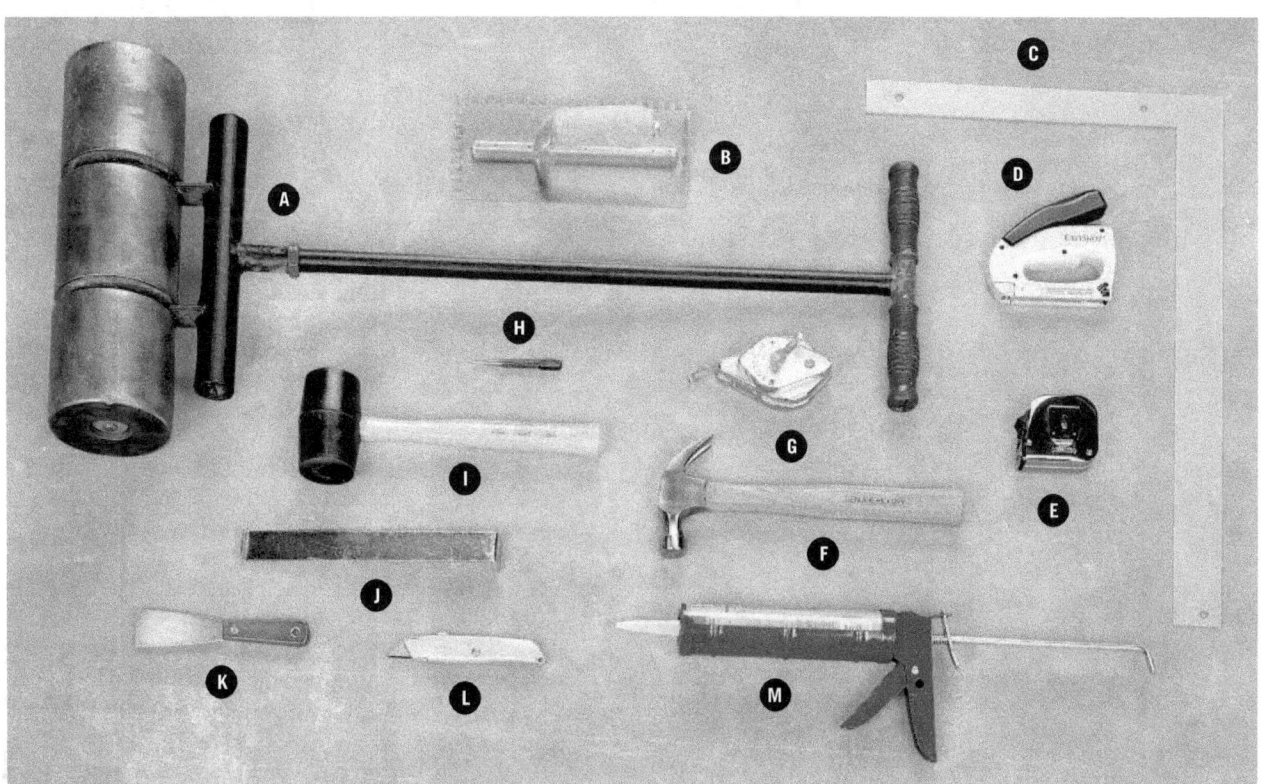

**Hand tools for hardwood flooring installation include:** floor roller (A), notched trowel (B), framing square (C), stapler (D), tape measure (E), hammer (F), chalk line (G), nail set (H), rubber mallet (I), floor pull bar (J), putty knife (K), utility knife (L), caulk gun (M).

INSTALLATION TECHNIQUES · 57

# Transitions for Hardwood Floors

At some point your wood floor will abut another flooring surface, a staircase, or a protrusion like a fireplace apron. Flooring manufacturers make a variety of transitions that match their products in composition and appearance for a flawless match.

When you install wood or laminate floors, the expansion gap between the perimeter of the floor and the walls needs to be covered with baseboards. If the existing baseboard is the basic ranch style, you may want to upgrade to a combination baseboard and shoe molding.

**Wood flooring transition** to tucked under carpet can be created by ripping a board to the necessary width, with the appropriate tongue or groove to mesh with the floor. Facenail to install.

**T-moldings** are available in several widths for wood floors and can be stained to match. Matching T-moldings are available for all laminate floors. T-moldings may be required for some floors at doorways to act as expansion joints. Fasten through the leg of the T. Some T-moldings require fastening a metal fixture to the subfloor. The T-molding then snaps into the fixture.

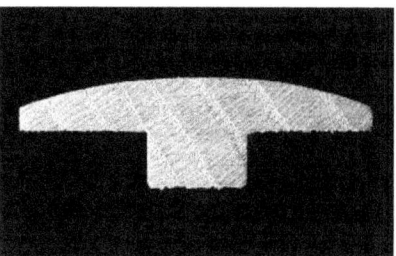

**T-molding** can be used to join any types of hard flooring so long as they are of equal height. Never use T-molding with carpet.

**Height-reducing thresholds** are used to transition between two floors of differing heights.

## THRESHOLDS AND MOLDINGS

A. **Carpet reducers** are used to finish off and create a smooth transition between hard flooring and carpeting.

B. **Stair nosing** is used to cover the exposed edges of stairs where the risers meet the steps. It is also used between step-downs and landings.

C. **Baby threshold** is used in place of baseboards and quarter round in front of sliding glass doors or door thresholds, to fill the gap between the floor and door.

D. **Reducer strips,** also called transition strips, are used between rooms when the floors are at different heights and are composed of different materials.

E. **Overlap reducers** are also used between rooms when one floor is at a different height than an adjoining room.

F. **T-moldings** are used to connect two floors of equal height. They are also used in doorways and thresholds to provide a smooth transition. T-moldings do not butt up against the flooring, allowing the wood to expand and contract under it.

G. **Baseboards** are used for almost all types of floors and are available in a wide variety of designs and thicknesses. They are applied at the bottom of walls to cover the gap between the floor and walls.

H. **Quarter round,** similar to shoe molding, is installed along the bottom edge of baseboard and sits on top of the floor. It covers any remaining gaps between the floor and walls.

# Options for Filling in Beneath a Removed Wall

**You may have a flooring gap** after a remodeling project that removes a wall, or you may want to interweave a new wood floor into a matching older floor.

Option 1

**Using the techniques outlined in How to Replace a Full Hardwood Plank** (page 145) remove the lengths of boards that abut the gap. If necessary, build up the subfloor in the patch area using layers of plywood and building paper to achieve the proper thickness. Install new boards as shown in the repair project.

Option 2

**Fill gaps in floors** with materials that have a contrasting color and pattern. For wood floors, parquet tiles are an easy and inexpensive choice. You may need to widen the gap with a circular saw set to the depth of the wood covering to make room for the contrasting tiles.

## TIP

**To enhance the effect,** cut away a border strip around the room and fill these areas with the same contrasting flooring material.

60  WOOD FLOORS

## STAIRCASE TIPS

If you want to have your stairs match your new flooring, you certainly can. Installing wood strips or laminate on stairs is not any more complicated than installing it on the flat floor. Here are a few tips:

- The horizontal part of the stair is called the tread and the vertical part is the riser. A closed staircase has walls on both sides. An open staircase has one or both sides open. Most stairs are created with a subfloor of risers and treads created either from 2× lumber or medium density fiberboard (MDF). If the subfloor treads have a nose, the nose will have to be sawn off to accommodate the new treads and risers.

- You will create new treads and risers using either strip flooring, engineered planks, or laminate. All flooring manufacturers make stair nosing to match their flooring products.

- Buy a stair width tool or stair tread jig. Inexpensive versions are available at major home improvement stores. This tool allows you to take accurate measurements of closed stairs, including the angles, since it is unlikely the treads are perfectly square.

- If the stairs were carpeted and have a nose, a protrusion on the tread that overhangs the riser, you need to saw off the existing nose. Use a circular saw against a guide to saw off most of the nose. Finish the cuts with a reciprocating saw. Sand off jagged edges if necessary.

- Install the risers first. Assemble strips or planks tall enough to be a riser. Use masking tape to hold them together. Use the stair measuring tool to determine width and cut to size and measure each riser separately (they may all be slightly different). Install all the risers first. Attach with high quality construction adhesive.

- On a closed stair, use the stair measuring tool to measure a tread width and cut a piece of nosing to fit. Dry fit the nosing on the tread and measure from the back of the nosing to the riser to get the depth of wood needed to cover the remaining tread. Cut to fit and dry fit all the pieces. Use masking tape to hold strips or planks together. Install with construction adhesive. Use yellow wood glue on the edge of the stair nose where it abuts the rest of the tread wood. Use a piece of 2 × 4 covered in carpet and a rubber mallet to set the pieces in the adhesive. Use a pneumatic nailer to drive four to six finish nails through the nosing into the subfloor.

- On an open staircase, the nosing will continue around the sides of the stair. Miter cut the nosings at 45° to create an attractive corner. Depending on the stair, you may need to cut a return for the back end of the side nosing.

**On open staircases,** miter the nosings at the corners.

# Wood Floor Installation Tips

Professional flooring installers have years of experience with various situations and materials. This wood floor might be the only one you install, so here are a few tips to increase your success.

Older subfloors were made of 1 × 6, 1 × 8, or even 1 × 10 planks typically installed diagonally across the joists. If your subfloor is planks, check that they are all firmly affixed to the joists. If not, attach them using ring-shank nails.

The long direction of your new flooring strips must run perpendicular to the floor joists. If your subfloor is plywood or oriented strandboard (OSB), you can install the flooring strips in whichever direction you choose, though in some cases you may need to add an additional layer of underlayment before beginning the installation.

**Tongues and grooves are there for a reason.** Uncut tongue-and-groove flooring has tongues and grooves across the ends as well as along the sides. If you remove the tongue across an end, that end should be facenailed. Some applications require gluing across the end tongues.

**Start with a high-quality subfloor.** A quality floor installation starts with a quality substrate. Make sure you have the appropriate thickness subfloor and underlayment for the product being used. Remove or fill any imperfections in the subfloor. Follow manufacturer's directions for using leveler or shimming.

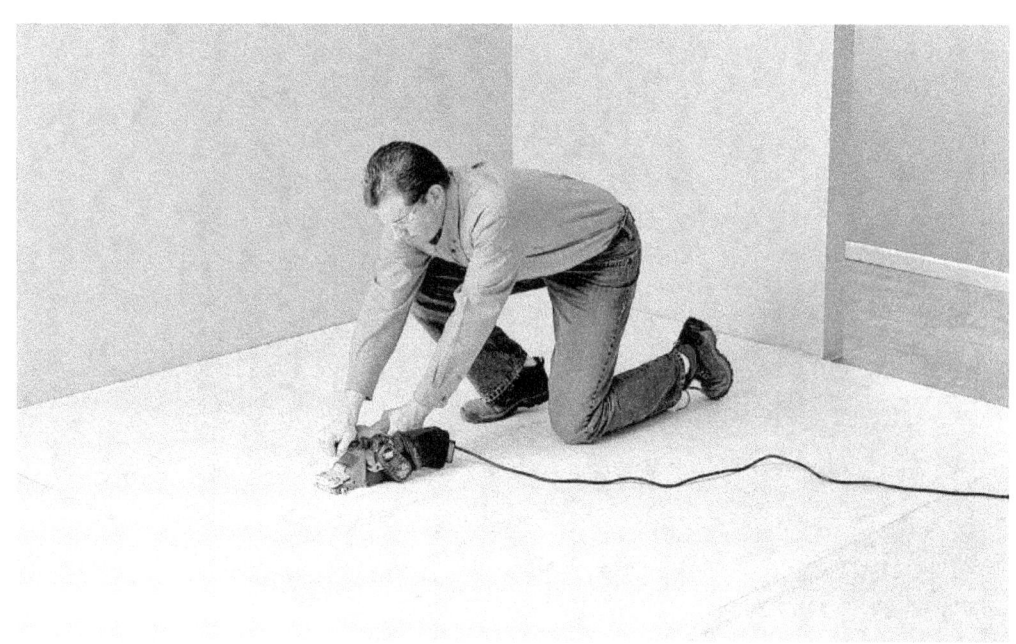

**Lay out the room.** Measure the width of the installation area and determine how many strips or planks will fit. The flooring piece dimensions are measured across the face of the piece, not including tongues. Lay out the floor so that the last piece at a transition or threshold is at least one half of the strip or plank width. Rip the initial strip to a width that will make the last strip at least one half width.

**Undercut door casing.** New flooring should be installed under door casings, not cut to fit around them. Use a piece of the new flooring, and underlayment if used, to determine the new flooring height. Use a flush cutting saw to cut the case molding. Cut flooring to fit around doorjambs or frames.

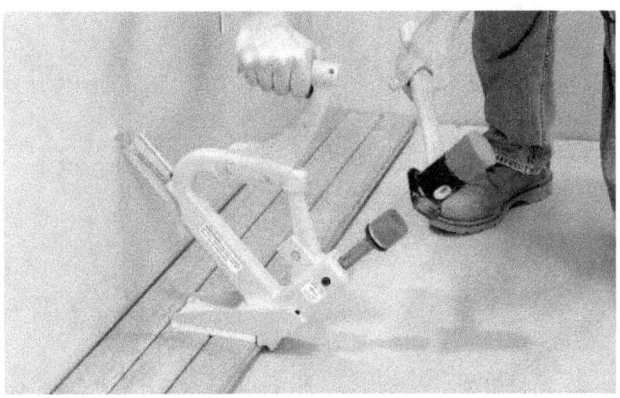

**Use the right tools.** The professionals use floor nailers, and not just because they are faster. A floor nailer, whether manual or pneumatic, drives the fastener at exactly the right angle and depth time after time. Take the time at the beginning of your project to adjust the depth. If applying adhesives, use the proper-sized trowel. Use the adhesive and the trowel size recommended by the flooring manufacturer.

**Check moisture content.** Tape 3' × 3' pieces of plastic over various locations on a concrete floor to test for moisture levels. If condensation accumulates on the plastic during the testing period, follow the manufacturer's recommended moisture-retarding techniques or install a raised subfloor. Use a moisture meter to check moisture content in wood subfloors.

**Clean concrete floors.** Adhesives will not adhere to concrete if any dirt, oil, or paint splatter is present. Use a power scrubber/buffer and the appropriate cleaner to clean the surface.

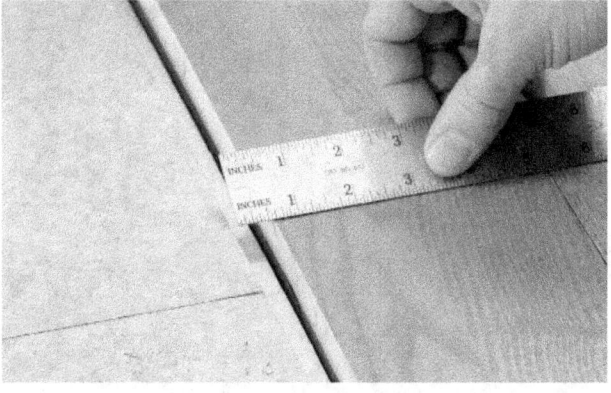

**Use expansion joints.** Installation of some floors over large areas (usually greater than 30' in any direction) may require an expansion joint. This joint allows the material to expand without buckling. Some expansion joints may be covered with a T-molding. Follow manufacturer's instructions for joint width.

# Wood Floor Installation

The projects in this chapter cover the most common installation techniques for hardwood and laminate floors.

All hardwood and laminate floor products are manufactured with tongue-and-groove joints. Whether you fasten the boards down with nails or glue, or whether the floor floats on a foam underlayment, the tongues and grooves hold the whole thing together.

Use the right tools and techniques, and you will find that wood floor installation might be one of the easiest and most rewarding home improvement projects you have done.

### In this chapter:
- Strip & Plank Floors
- Bonded Bamboo Strip Flooring
- Installing Laminate Flooring

# Strip & Plank Floors

## TOOLS & MATERIALS

| | | |
|---|---|---|
| Jigsaw | Hammer | Eye and ear protection |
| Circular saw | Pry bar | Work gloves |
| Stapler | Power nailer | **For bonded floor:** |
| Utility knife | Rosin paper | Notched trowel |
| Tape measure | Wood floor strips or planks | Flooring adhesive |
| Chalk line | Nails or staples | Wood glue |
| Drill | Reducer strip or transition strip | Cardboard |
| Flooring pull bar | Nail set | Floor roller |
| Rubber mallet | Wood putty | |

Installing tongue-and-groove hardwood strips or planks is straightforward. They can be fastened with mechanical fasteners such as nails or staples, or they can be glued down or fully bonded. Regardless of installation methods, strips, planks, or engineered planks must run perpendicular to the joists unless additional underlayment has been installed. Be sure to measure and cut boards at the appropriate ends to ensure the tongue-and-groove joints fit together for end matches.

To fasten with mechanical fasteners, the first and last boards are facenailed, while the other boards are blind-nailed through the tongue. Once the first few rows are installed, use a power nailer—either manual or pneumatic. The power nailer positions the fastener at exactly the right angle through the tongue, the body of the board, and into the floor. It is critical that the nail depth is set correctly. The fastener should be set slightly below the surface of the tongue. If it is set above or flush with the surface, it may cause dimpling in the finished floor. If the staple or nail penetrates more than halfway through the tongue, the board will creak or squeak. To set the fastener depth correctly, fasten a sample board to the subfloor/underlayment. Once you have adjusted the depth, fasten

a second board to check for consistency. Once set, remove the sample boards and destroy.

A fully bonded wood floor is attached to the subfloor with adhesive, much like a tile floor. A bonded wood floor can be installed over concrete and tile, and is typically used over radiant heating systems so the heating elements are not punctured by fasteners. The flooring product, adhesive, and subfloor and underlayment must all be compatible. The instructions that come with your floor cover all the appropriate combinations.

# How to Install a Hardwood Plank Floor

**Acclimate the flooring** by stacking planks in the installation room. Separate the rows of flooring with wood scraps. Allow the material to rest in the space for several days, or as directed by the manufacturer's instructions.

**TIP:** Inspect the wood flooring as soon as it arrives. Look for any major defects such as knots, cracks, and damaged, warped, or bowed boards. It's easier to replace inadequate boards during the acclimation period than in mid-installation.

**Install a layer of rosin paper over the entire subfloor,** stapling it down and overlapping the edges by 4". The purpose of this layer is mostly to eliminate noise caused by the floorboards scraping or pressing on the wood subfloor or underlayment (if required), which should be installed and leveled before the flooring installation begins (pages 44 to 47).

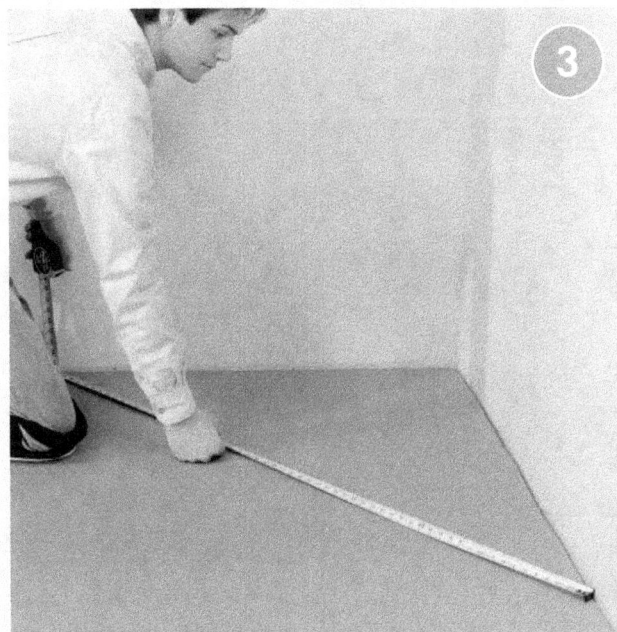

**Check that the room is square** using the 3-4-5 rule: measure out 3' from a corner in one direction and 4' in the other direction—the distance between the marks should be exactly 5'. If the room is out of square, you'll have to decide which wall (usually the longest) to follow as a baseline for laying the flooring.

**Determine the location of the floor joist** and drive a nail in at each end, centered on the joists. Snap chalk lines along the centerlines of each joist, connecting the nails. Use these as a reference for installing floorboards.

*(continued)*

WOOD FLOOR INSTALLATION

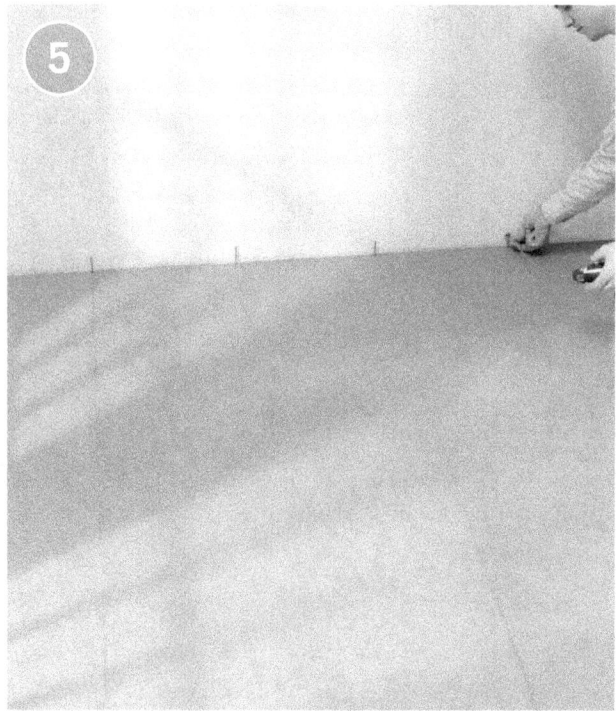

**Snap a starter line.** Measure ¾" out from the longest wall, perpendicular to the floor joists, to allow for an expansion gap. Drive a nail at each end, and snap a chalk line parallel to the wall.

**Drive spacer nails,** such as 8d finish nails, every 4 to 5" along the chalk line, as a guide for placement of the first row of planks. Drive the nails in far enough to be stable, but with enough of the nail protruding to serve as a bumper for the flooring (and to make the nail easier to remove later).

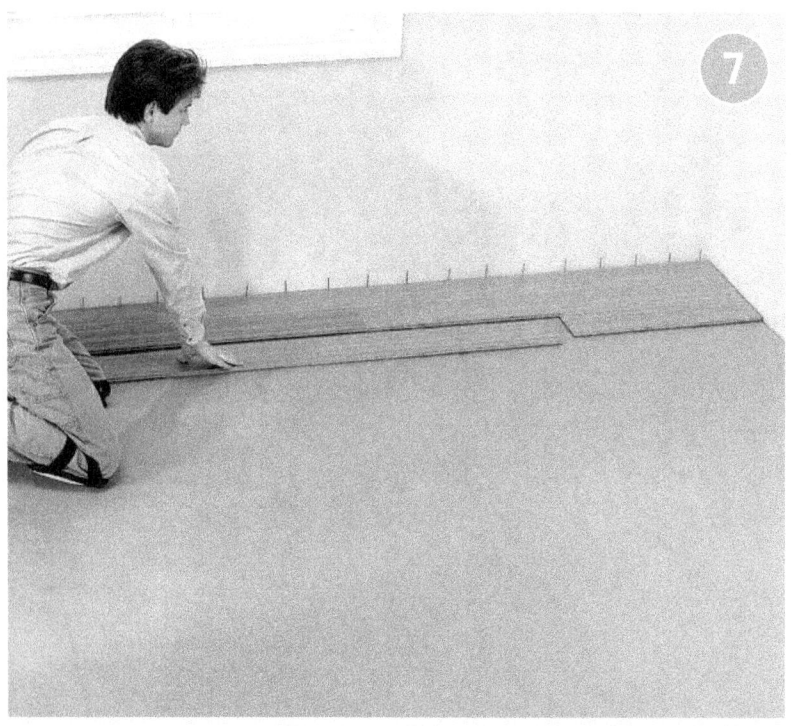

**Lay down a dry run for the first two or three rows** to determine plank positions for best appearance. Mark the backs of planks with a pencil to keep them in your preferred order and remove them from the work area. Make sure the end joints are staggered by more than 6" apart on adjoining planks. Create a lay out that has perimeter pieces that are longer than 6".

**VARIATION:** Some manufacturers recommend that you apply a bead of flooring adhesive to the backs of wider planks prior to nailing them. Use the recommended adhesive and lay beads across the width of the plank; keep adhesive at least ½" from the edges and 1½" from the ends.

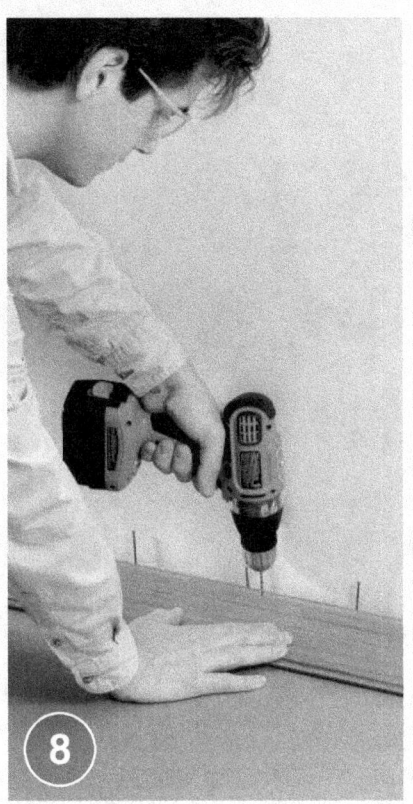

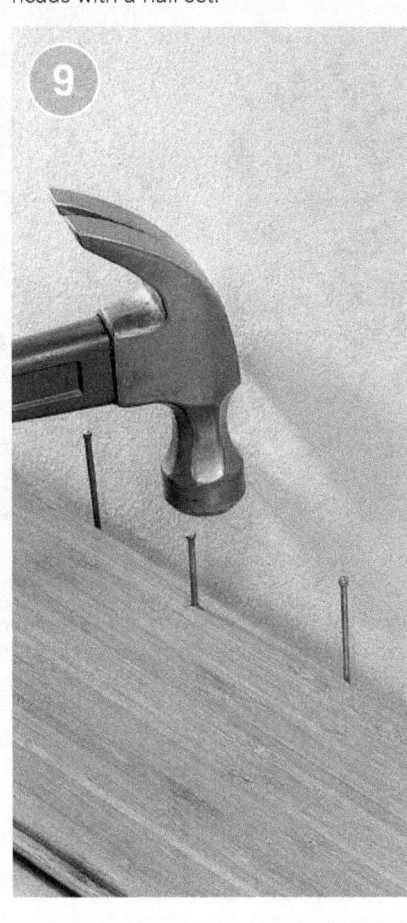

**Attach the first floorboards** by facenailing 8d finish nails into the pilot holes along the wall edge. Sink the nail heads with a nail set.

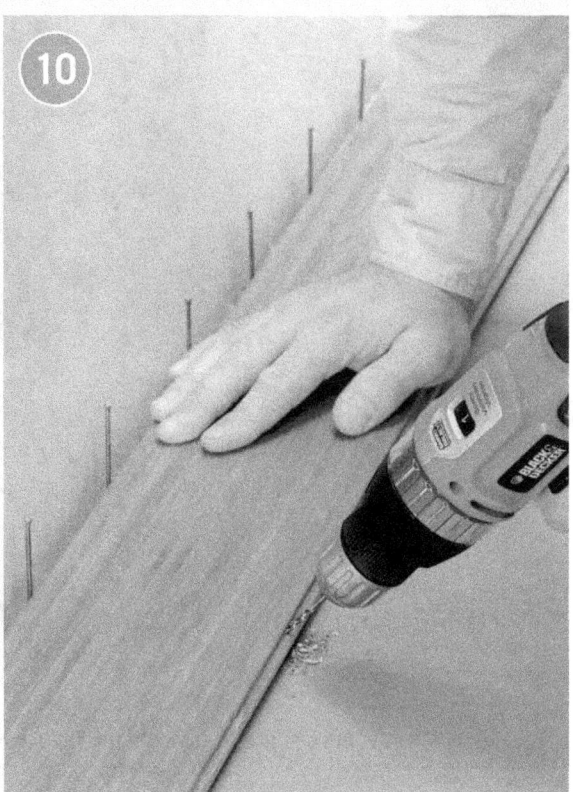

**Install the first row.** Choose the longest planks available for this row. Lay the planks in place and drill holes every 8" for facenailing along the wall edge. Locate the holes ¼ to ½" in from the edge, where they'll be covered up by the base molding and shoe.

**Pre-drill pilot holes** through the tongues of the first row planks and blind-nail 8d finish or flooring nails. Make sure the heads of the nails do not stick up through the tops of the tongues, where they would interfere with the tongue-and-groove joint.

##  PLUGGING COUNTERBORES

Wider plank floors frequently require that you fasten the ends of floorboards by screwing down through the board and into the subfloor. This is most commonly needed when you are installing wood flooring that does not have tongue-and-groove ends. In such cases, drill counterbored pilot holes for the screws, making sure the counterbores are deep enough to accept a wood plug. After the floorboards are installed, check to make sure the screws are tight (but be careful not to overdrive them) and then glue a wood plug into each counterbore. Wood plugs should be the same species as the flooring or, if that's not available, make them a contrasting species. See page 103 for how to cut plugs. Sand the plugs so the tops are even with surrounding floor and finish them at the same time.

**NOTE:** If you are using matching plugs, orient them in the counterbores with the wood grain running parallel to the floorboards; if you are using contrasting plugs, make the grains perpendicular.

*(continued)*

WOOD FLOOR INSTALLATION • 69

**Cut the end planks for each row to length,** so that the butt end faces the wall. In other words, try and preserve the tongue-and-groove profiles if your flooring has them on the ends. Saw the planks with a fine-tooth blade, making sure to orient the workpiece so you'll be cutting into the face, minimizing tearout on the surface.

**After the second row,** use a flooring nailer to blind-nail the tongues of each plank. Flooring nailers are struck with a mallet to drive and set the flooring nails through the floorboard tongues. They can be rented at most home centers or rental centers.

**NOTE:** You can continue to hand-nail if you choose, but it is difficult to get the same consistency, and it is certainly more painstaking. Be sure to continue pre-drilling pilot holes as well to avoid damaging the tongues.

**Keep joints tight.** As you install each successive plank in a row, use a flooring pull bar at the open end of the plank. Drive the end of the board toward the joint by rapping on the pull bar with a mallet.

**At the end of rows and along walls,** use a pull bar to seat the boards. For the last row, rip the planks as necessary, use the pull bar to seat them, and facenail along the edge as you did with the first row.

**If a plank is slightly bowed,** cut fitting wedges to force the wayward board into position before nailing it. Make wedges by cutting two triangles from a 1' or longer scrap of flooring (inset). Attach one half of the wedge pair with the outside edge parallel to the bowed plank. Slide the groove of the other wedge piece onto the tongue of the bowed plank, and hammer until the plank sits flush against its neighbor. Nail the plank into place. Remove the wedge parts.

**Install a reducer strip or other transition** as needed between the plank floor and adjoining rooms. Cut the strip to size and fit the strip's groove over the plank's tongue. Drill pilot holes and facenail the strip with 8d finishing nails. Sink the nails with a nail set, putty, and sand smooth.

**Install a quarter-round shoe molding** to cover all the expansion gaps between the floor and walls at the edge of the floor. Paint, stain, or finish the molding before installing.

**To reverse the direction of the tongue and groove** at doorways or other openings, glue a spline into the groove of the plank. Fit the groove of the following board onto the spline and nail into place as before.

WOOD FLOOR INSTALLATION

## How to Install a Fully Bonded Wood Strip Floor

**To establish a straight layout line,** snap a chalk line parallel to the longest wall, about 30" from the wall. Kneel in this space to begin flooring installation.

**Apply flooring adhesive to the subfloor** on the other side of the layout line with a notched trowel, according to the manufacturer's directions. Take care not to obscure the layout line with adhesive.

**Apply wood glue to the grooved end of each piece** as you install it to help joints stay tight. Do not apply glue to the long sides of boards.

**Install the first row of flooring** with the edge of the tongues directly over the chalk line. Make sure end joints are tight, then wipe up any excess glue immediately. At walls, leave a ½" space to allow for expansion of the wood. This gap will be covered by moldings.

**For succeeding rows,** insert the tongue into the groove of the preceding row, and pivot the flooring down into the adhesive. Gently slide the tongue and groove ends together. At walls, use a hammer and a flooring pull bar to draw together the joints on the last strip (inset).

**After you've installed three or four rows,** use a mallet and scrap piece of flooring to gently tap boards together, closing up the seams. All joints should fit tightly.

**Use a cardboard template to fit boards in irregular areas.** Cut cardboard to match the space and allow for a ½" expansion gap next to the wall. Trace the template outline on a board, then cut it to fit using a jigsaw. Finish laying strips over the entire floor.

**Bond the flooring to the adhesive** by rolling it with a heavy floor roller. Roll the flooring within 3 hours of the adhesive application. Work in sections, and finish by installing the flooring in the section between your starting line and the wall.

WOOD FLOOR INSTALLATION

# Bonded Bamboo Strip Flooring

It looks like hardwood and is available in traditional tongue-and-groove form and in laminate planks. But bamboo is not wood. It's really a grass—and one of the most popular flooring materials today.

Bamboo flooring is made by shredding stalks of the raw material, then pressing them together with a resin that holds the shreds in their finished shape. Not only is bamboo a fast-growing and renewable crop, the companies that make bamboo flooring use binders with low emissions of volatile organic compounds (VOCs). The result is tough, economical, and ecologically friendly. In other words, it's just about perfect for flooring.

If you choose tongue-and-groove bamboo, the installation techniques are the same as for hardwoods. Bamboo is also available as a snap-fit laminate for use in floating floors. In this project we use thin, durable planks that are glued to the underlayment (see Resources, page 155).

### TOOLS & MATERIALS

| | |
|---|---|
| Adhesive | Weighted roller |
| Carpenter's level | Bamboo flooring material |
| Carpenter's square | Hammer |
| Chalk line | Drill |
| Cleaning supplies | Screws |
| Marking pen or pencil | Nails |
| Measuring tape | Circular saw |
| Moisture level meter | Butcher paper |
| Notched trowel | Weights |
| Rubber mallet | Trim |
| Scrap lumber | Floor leveler (if necessary) |
| Shims | Sandpaper |
| Straightedge | Eye protection and gloves |

### TIPS FOR SUCCESSFUL INSTALLATION

Bamboo plank flooring should be one of the last items installed on any new construction or remodeling project. All work involving water or moisture should be completed before floor installation. Room temperature and humidity of installation area should be consistent with normal, year-round living conditions for at least a week before installation. Room temperature of 60 to 70°F and a humidity range of 40 to 60% is recommended.

About radiant heat: The subfloor should never exceed 85°F. Check the manufacturer's suggested guidelines for correct water temperature inside heating pipes. Switch on the heating unit three days before flooring installation. Room temperature should not vary more than 15°F year-round. For glue-down installations, leave the heating unit on for three days following installation.

WOOD FLOOR INSTALLATION • 75

# How to Install Bonded Bamboo Strip Flooring

**Give the bamboo time to adjust to installation conditions.** Store it for at least 72 hours in or near the room where it will be installed. Open the packages for inspection, but do not store the planks on concrete or near outside walls.

**Even though thin-plank bamboo is an engineered material,** it can vary in appearance. Buy all planks from the same lot and batch number. Then inspect the planks to make sure they match. Use the same lighting as you will have in the finished room.

**Inspect the underlayment.** Bamboo planks can be installed on plywood or oriented strand board at least ¾" thick. The underlayment must be structurally sound; wood surfaces should have no more than 12% moisture.

**Make sure the underlayment is level.** It should not change by more than ⅛" over 10'. If necessary, apply a floor leveler to fill any low places, and sand down any high spots. Prevent squeaks by driving screws every 6" into the subfloor below.

**Sweep and vacuum the surface,** then measure all room dimensions.

**Check corners for squareness** using the 3-4-5 triangle method. (See page 67.)

**The planks should be perpendicular to the floor joists below.** Adjust your starting point if necessary. Snap a chalk line next to the longest wall. The distance from the wall should be the same at both ends, leaving ½" for expansion.

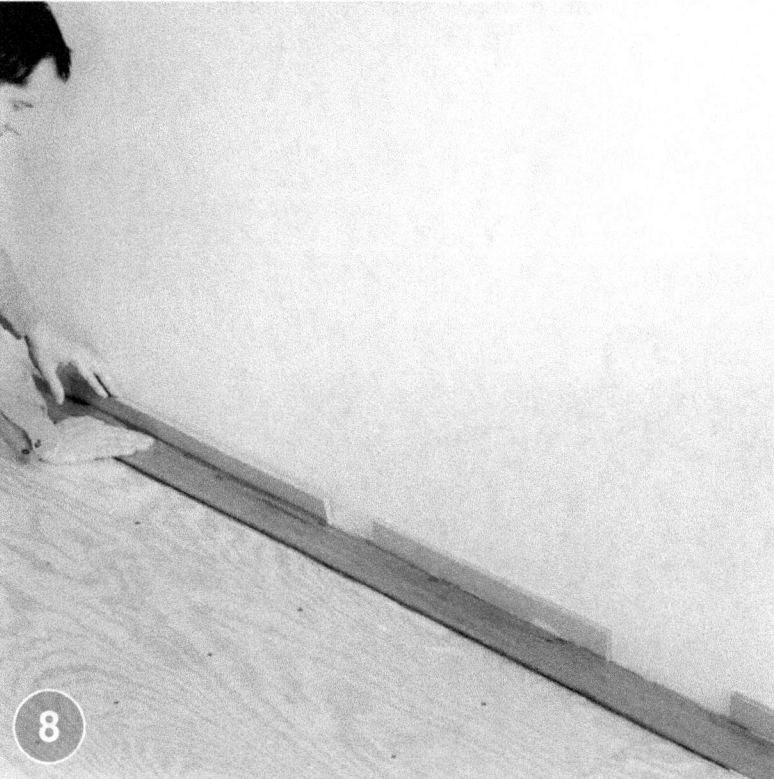

**Lay the first course of planks** with the tongue edge toward the wall. Align the planks with the chalk line. Hold the edge course in place with wedges, or by nailing through the tongue edge. This row will anchor the others, so make sure it stays securely in place. *(continued)*

WOOD FLOOR INSTALLATION • 77

**Once the starter row is in place,** install the planks using a premium wood flooring adhesive. Be sure to follow the manufacturer's instructions. Begin at the chalk line and apply enough adhesive to lay down one or two rows of planks. Spread the adhesive with a V-notched trowel at a 45° angle. Let the adhesive sit for the specified time.

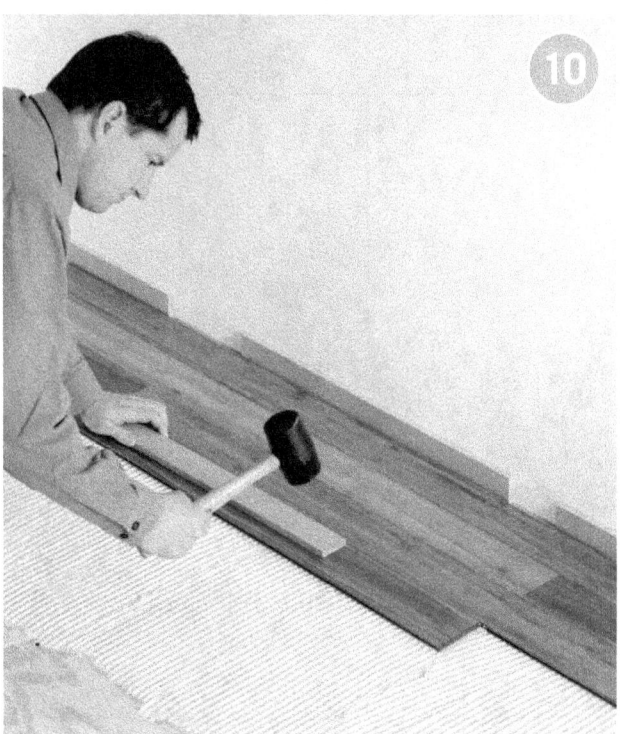

**When the adhesive is tacky and ready to use,** lay the first section of bamboo planks. Set each plank in the adhesive by placing a clean piece of scrap lumber on top and tapping it down with a rubber mallet. Check the edge of each section to make sure it keeps a straight line.

**After you finish the first section,** cover the next area with adhesive and give it time to become tacky. Waiting for the adhesive to become tacky is necessary, even though it slows your work down—and it allows the section you just finished to set up.

**When the adhesive is ready,** lay down the next section of planks. Fit the new planks tightly against the previous section, taking care not to knock the finished section out of alignment. If the planks have tongue-and-groove edges, fit them carefully into place.

**Continue applying adhesive and installing planks,** one section at a time, to cover the entire floor. When adhesive gets on the flooring surface, wipe it off quickly.

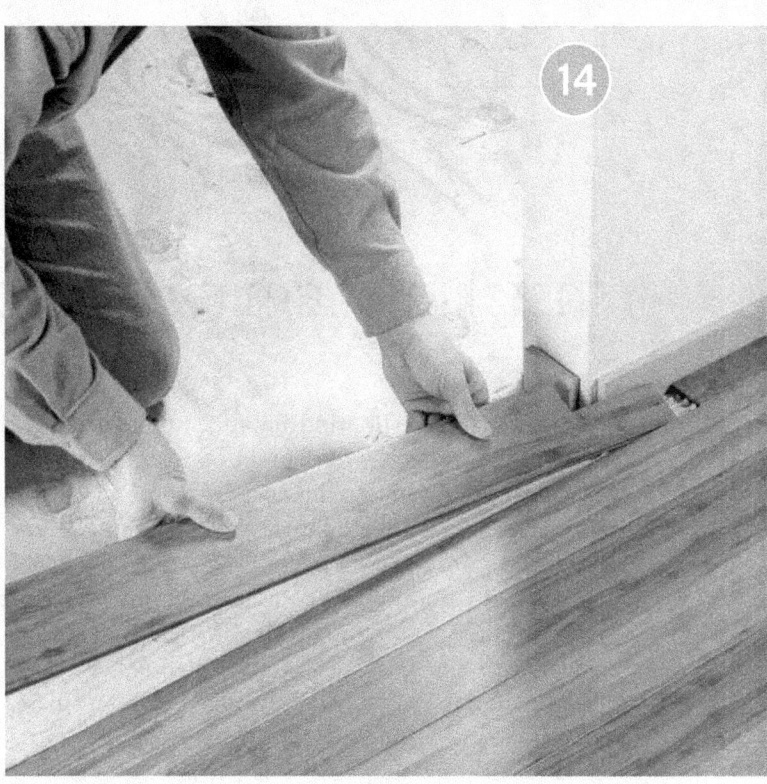

**At the edges and around any fixed objects,** such as doorways or plumbing pipes, leave a ½" gap for expansion. Use shims to maintain the gaps if needed. These spaces can be covered with baseboards, base shoe, and escutcheons.

**As you finish each section,** walk across it a few times to maximize contact between the planks and the adhesive. When all the planks are in place, clean the surface and use a clean weighted roller. Push the roller in several directions, covering the entire surface many times.

**In places that are difficult to reach with a roller,** lay down a sheet of protective material, such as butcher paper, and stack weights on the paper. Let the finished floor sit for at least 24 hours, then clean the surface and remove any spacers from the expansion gaps. Finally, install the finishing trim.

# Installing Laminate Flooring

Most big-name flooring manufacturers now feature dozens if not hundreds of laminate flooring options among their catalogues, for a very simple reason: laminates are favorites among DIYers and value-conscious shoppers.

Laminate flooring is a multilayer synthetic product in which the layers are fused (laminated) together. The core of the flooring is usually a high-density fiberboard (HDF) that is tightly bonded with resins. To this core, a photo appliqué layer is bonded—this layer is not wood at all, but a plastic layer that can be made to look remarkably like any kind of wood. Over the plastic photo later is a clear protective surface layer that protects against wear.

The technology makes it possible for the flooring to closely resemble any desired wood simply by varying the photo appliqué layer. Recent advances even allow the laminate products to be textured in a way that closely mimics actual wood grain. Laminate flooring products are very stable and easy to install, making them an excellent choice for DIYers.

Laminate flooring products have few drawbacks, but they can be susceptible to scratching, especially in high traffic areas, and they are not always the best choice for high moisture areas, such as bathrooms or laundry rooms. And there have been cases of lower-quality, non-brand-name flooring products that delaminate over time.

You can minimize the chances for problems by buying a quality product from a well-known, reputable manufacturer, and checking the product specifications to make sure it is appropriate for your planned location. Most manufacturers offer products marketed as "waterproof" or "water-resistant" for bathrooms and other wet locations, though you should be aware that these will never be quite as genuinely waterproof as ceramic tile or vinyl floor.

Early laminate flooring products were installed with a full glue-down bond to the subfloor, and while some of these products are still available, the vast majority of laminate floors are now installed with a "floating" system that requires no glue. A locking channel system holds the planks together both along the length and at the ends, and simple gravity holds the flooring down.

Because laminate floors float, foot traffic can create a hollow sound as the flooring flexes under footsteps. This is one reason why all manufacturers require that the flooring be installed on a special underlayment that deadens the sound and minimizes the flexing of the floor. Some flooring products have the resilient foam underlayment already attached to the bottom of the flooring planks.

Be aware that if you are installing your flooring on concrete, some form of additional moisture barrier is necessary before the underlayment and flooring are laid. Without it, moisture seeping up from below could loosen the bond of the laminate fibers, eventually ruining your floor. Closely follow the manufacturer's recommendations for this, and when installing over a concrete slab, make sure to lay down whatever moisture barrier is recommended. Some sheet underlayments are two-ply, with a moisture barrier under the resilient foam layer.

Installation instructions vary slightly from manufacturer to manufacturer, but the principles are very much the same, and the instructions here should be sufficient for most of the name-brand products you might buy. The product we're using calls for a sheet underlayment to be laid down first. As with any DIY project, read the following pages carefully and make sure you understand everything before you begin.

Laminate floors are intended to expand and contract by small amounts in response to temperature and humidity changes. This means that the flooring is installed with a small gap around the walls—the gap is covered by shoe moldings attached against the baseboards. Our product requires a ⅜-inch gap around all walls; your product may have a slightly different recommendation.

An important first step is to unpack your flooring and allow it to acclimate to the conditions of your room before beginning installation. Do not bypass this step.

Before

After

WOOD FLOOR INSTALLATION

**These samples of laminates sold at major home improvement centers** show the enormous variety of looks that are available. Today's laminate floors require close inspection to distinguish them from genuine wood.

## TOOLS & MATERIALS

| | | |
|---|---|---|
| Eye & ear protection | Jigsaw | Hammer |
| Work gloves | Hole saw | Level |
| Utility knife | Pull bar | Liquid floor leveler (if necessary) |
| Tape measure | Tapping block | Nails (as needed) |
| Power miter saw | Rubber mallet | Sheet underlayment kit with clear tape |
| Circular saw | Rubber gloves | Laminate flooring |
| Pry bar | Compass | Flooring spacers |

## How to Prepare the Floor for Laminate Flooring

**Remove baseboard shoe moldings** using a small pry bar. If your trim style does not include shoe moldings, as is the case if you have ranch-style moldings, remove the entire baseboard molding. Carefully removed baseboards can be easily reinstalled.

**Remove the old flooring, if necessary** (see page 38). Before continuing with preparation, unpack the flooring and stack it in the room being floored, to allow the temperature and moisture levels to stabilize.

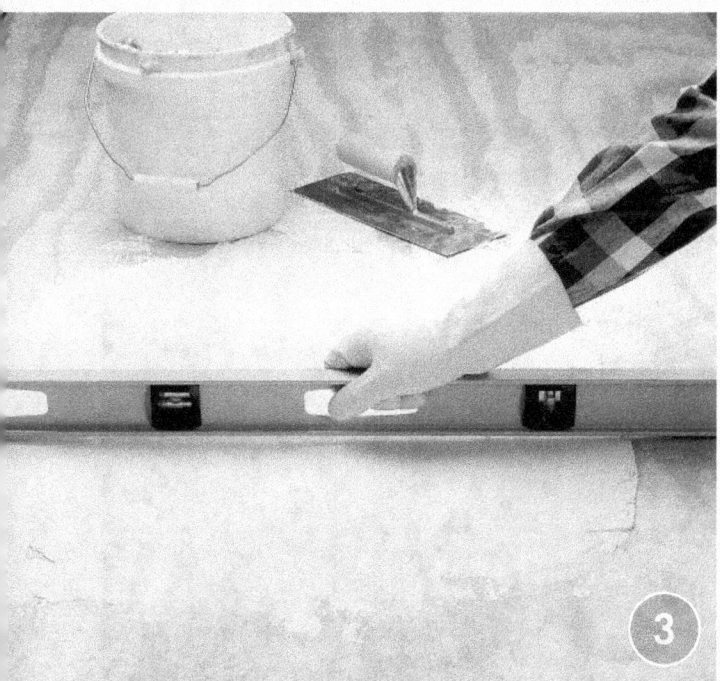

**Using a long level or other straightedge,** check the floor for dips or crowns, and if necessary correct these. Loose underlayment can be nailed down, and small dips can be leveled out with liquid floor leveler.

**OPTION:** On concrete, install a DRIcore subfloor to raise the new floor slightly above the slab (see page 48).

**Using a prybar and hammer,** loosen and pry up the tackstrip that held the carpet in place. The tackstrip may break apart as you work; use care to avoid injuring yourself on the sharp tacks.

*(continued)*

WOOD FLOOR INSTALLATION • 83

**Plan the layout.** Measure the width of the room and subtract ¾" to accommodate the ⅜" gap needed along each wall. Now, divide this number by the width of the flooring planks to arrive at the number of rows of flooring you will need. If the resulting number of rows gives you a partial fraction that is more than ½ the plank width, rip planks for the first row to this measurement. But if the partial fraction is less than ½ the plank width, then divide this measurement by 2, and plan to rip both the first and the last rows to this measurement. The goal is to avoid a very narrow strip on one side of the room only.

**Install the required sheet underlayment.** Cut the underlayment sheets to fit using a utility knife, then tape sheets together to cover the floor using clear tape. (Some underlayment products unfold, with self-adhesive edges.) Follow manufacturer's recommendation for overlap between sheets.

**NOTE:** On concrete floors, you will need to install a 6-mil sheet plastic vapor barrier, then the sheet underlayment; or install a DRIcore raised underlayment.

**Install ⅜"-thick spacers** around each wall, spaced every 2'. A flooring installation kit specified by your manufacturer may have these spacers included; or, you can trim wood shims to this thickness and use them as spacers.

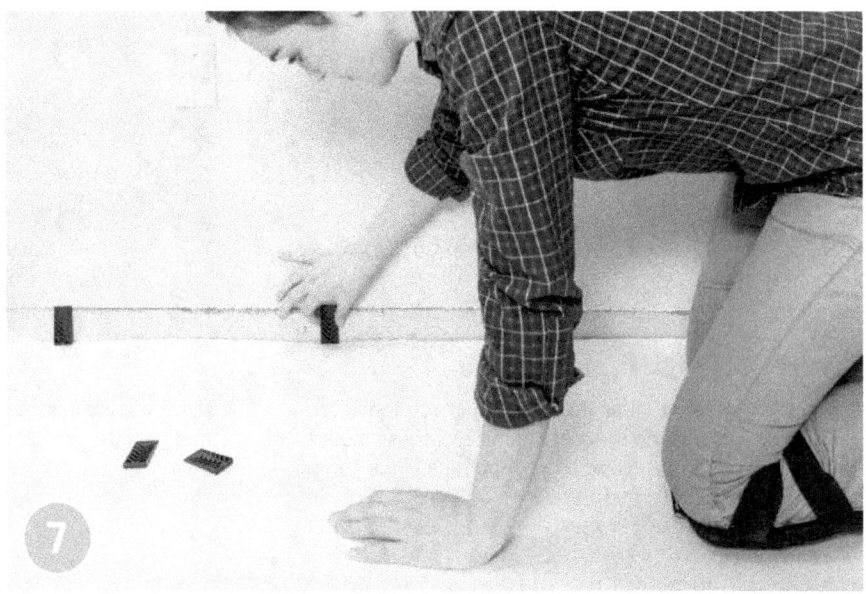

# How to Install a Floating Laminate Floor

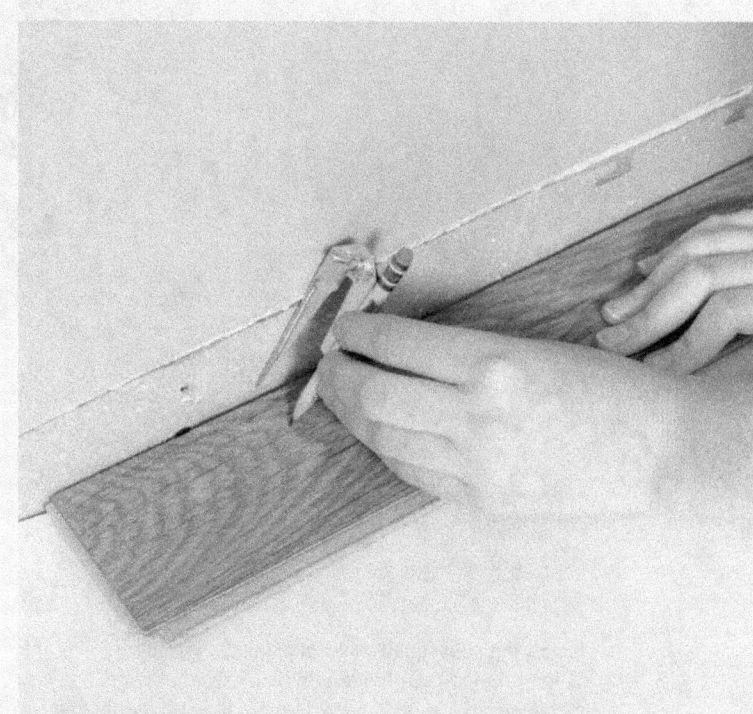

**Inspect each plank,** and reject any that are scarred or that have damaged tongues or grooves. For the first row of planks along the wall, remove the tongues along the long sides of the planks using a circular saw or table saw.

**NOTE:** If you are ripping the first row down to accommodate a partial plank, then make sure to cut away the tongue-side of the plank.

**VARIATION:** If your wall is irregular, using a compass to trace the wall outline on the plank, then use a jigsaw to cut the plank to conform to the wall's contours.

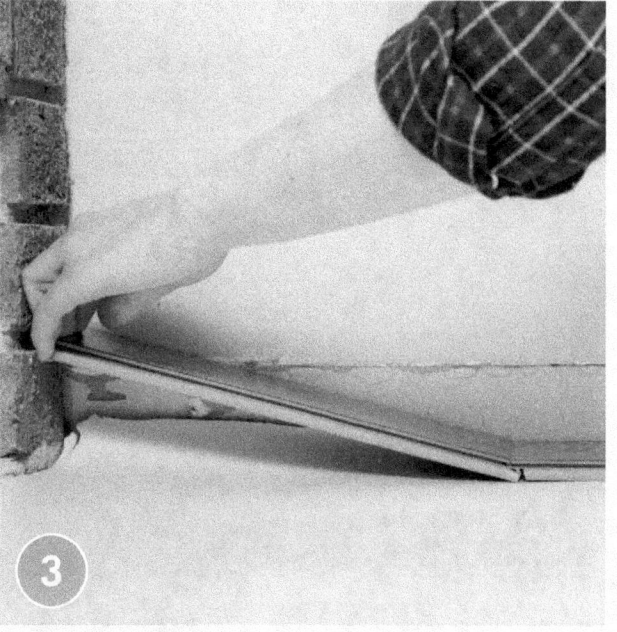

**Cross-cut a plank into ⅓- and ⅔-length segments.** These pieces will be used to start the second and third rows, respectively.

**Begin laying the first row** using the planks with the tongues cut away, beginning with a full-length piece in the corner. Make sure to maintain a ⅜" gap along both walls. For the second piece, align the end tongue-and-groove, and snap into place. At the last plank in the row, cut the plank to fit with a miter saw, maintaining the ⅜" gap to the wall. *(continued)*

WOOD FLOOR INSTALLATION

**Install the subsequent rows of planks,** alternating full plank, ⅔-length plank, and ⅓-length plank, so that joints are staggered in a repeating pattern. To fit each plank, first insert the tongue into the edge groove of the previous row of planks, then slide it laterally until the new plank butts up to the end of the preceding piece. Snap downward to lock into place.

**If necessary, tap on the opposite end of the plank** with a tapping block to snug up the joint. Take care, though, not to damage the plank.

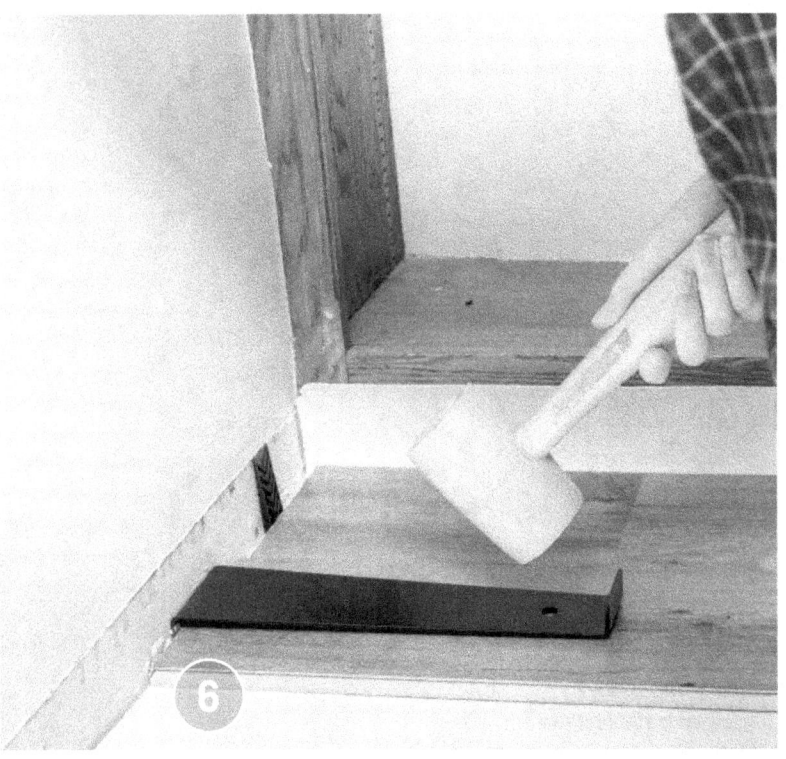

**At the last piece in the row, cut length to size,** then fit the piece into the edge groove, and use the pull bar and hammer to lightly draw the piece back to secure the end joint.

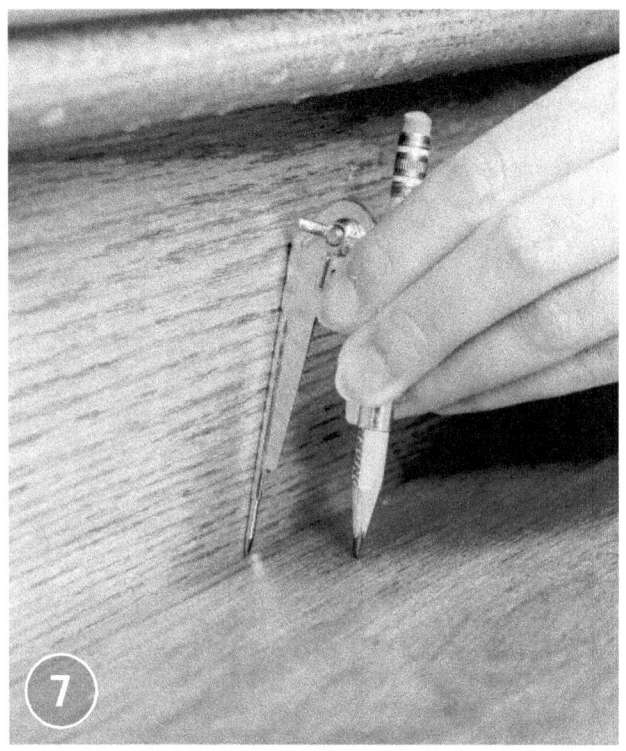

**As you install the last row,** lay each full piece against the wall on top of the last installed piece, with a scrap plank positioned vertically against the wall as a spacer. Trace the wall contour onto the plank.

**Cut along the scribed lines** of the last planks using a jigsaw.

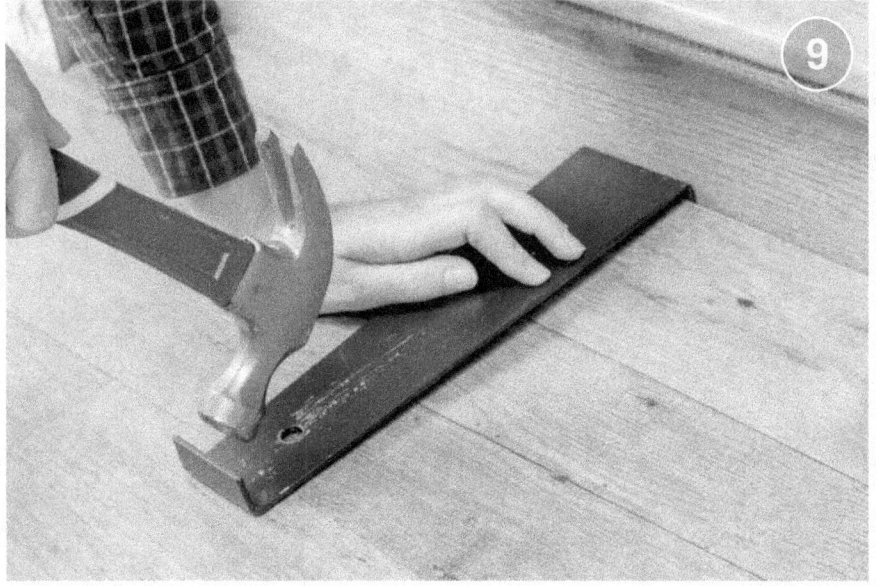

**To install the pieces of the final row,** slide the long-side tongue into the groove of the previous row, with the ends aligned. Use the pull bar and hammer to work along the length of the plank, pulling toward you to gently secure the joint.

**Reinstall the trim moldings** that were removed, covering the gaps between the flooring and the wall. Remember the floating floor needs to expand and contract, so make sure to drive finish nails at an angle into the wall, not into the flooring.

## How to Cut Laminate Flooring for Openings & Obstacles

**For pipes, carefully measure and mark where the opening will be,** by aligning the piece to be installed against the obstacle and marking with a pencil. Make sure to add a ⅜" expansion gap around all sides. Then, cut the opening with a hole saw. Extend the notch to the edges of the plank using a jigsaw.

**For internal cutouts, such as those required for floor ducts,** first outline the opening on the laminate plank. Drill small corner holes as pilot openings, then use a jigsaw to cut out the opening. Because jigsaws cut on the upstroke, orient the workpiece with the underside facing up to prevent tearout as you cut.

# Special Floor Projects

Not every floor is installed in strips, and not every wood floor is new. These wood floor projects are special installations that build on the techniques of standard installation but add a few twists.

Parquet floors look beautiful and might seem unattainable, but installing parquet is as simple as snapping a few guidelines and spreading some adhesive. Also easy to install and absolutely stunning are floor medallions. And, given that medallion manufacturers will create medallions in any look you desire, you can have the most custom of custom floors.

Reusing and recycling are trending, and you can use various reclaimed woods to create your wood floor.

In this chapter:
- Parquet Tile
- Decorative Medallion
- Vintage Wood Floors
- End Grain Floors
- One-Piece Molding
- Built-Up Molding

# Parquet Tile

## TOOLS & MATERIALS

Tape measure
Chalk line
Parquet flooring
Adhesive
Notched trowel
Putty knife
Rubber mallet
100- to 150-pound floor roller
Jigsaw
Circular saw
Paper
Scissors
½" spacers
Eye and ear protection
Rubber gloves

For a hardwood floor with greater design appeal, consider installing parquet. It offers more visual interest than strip flooring without sacrificing the beauty and elegance of wood. Parquet comes in a variety of patterns and styles to create geometric designs. It can range from elaborate, custom-designed patterns on the high end, to the more common herringbone pattern or the widely available and less expensive block design. The finger block pattern is one of the most widely available parquet coverings and also one of the least expensive. The configuration of perpendicular strips of wood in this design emphasizes the different grains and natural color variations.

Parquet has experienced a radical transformation over the years. A few years ago, each individual piece of parquet was hand-cut and painstakingly assembled piece by piece. Today, parquet is prefabricated so the individual pieces making up the design are available as single tiles, which has not only reduced the cost, but has made the flooring easier to install as well. The effort can be very rewarding: parquet can be used to create shapes and decorations not possible with other wood flooring.

**Parquetry adds depth and pattern** to your decor and is an excellent choice for formal and informal spaces.

# How to Install Parquet Tiles

**Mark the centerpoint of each wall.** Snap chalk lines between the marks on opposite walls to establish your reference lines. Use the 3-4-5 triangle method to check the lines for squareness.

**Lay out a dry run of panels** from the center point along the reference lines to adjacent walls. If more than half of the last panel needs to be cut off, adjust the lines by half the width of the panel. Snap new working lines, if necessary.

**Apply enough adhesive onto the subfloor** for your first panel using a putty knife. Spread the adhesive into a thin layer with a notched trowel held at a 45° angle. Apply the adhesive right up to the working lines, but do not cover them.

**Place the first panel on the adhesive** so two sides are flush with the working lines. Take care not to slide or twist the panel when setting it into place. This panel must be positioned correctly to keep the rest of your floor square. *(continued)*

SPECIAL FLOOR PROJECTS • 93

**Apply enough adhesive for six to eight panels** and spread it with a notched trowel.

**Set the next panel in place** by holding it at a 45° angle and locking the tongue-and-groove joints with the first panel. Lower the panel onto the adhesive without sliding it. Install remaining panels the same way.

**After every six to eight panels are installed,** tap them into the adhesive with a rubber mallet.

**For the last row,** place a panel directly on top of the last installed row. Place a third panel on top of this, with the sides butted against ½" spacers along the wall. Draw a line along the edge of the third panels onto the second row, cut the panels at the marks, and install.

**To work around corners or obstacles,** align a panel over the last installed panel, then place another panel on top of it as in step 8. Keep the top panel ½" from the wall or obstacle and trace along the opposite edge onto the second panel (top). Move the top two panels to the adjoining side, making sure not to turn the top panel. Make a second mark on the panel the same way (bottom). Cut the tile with a jigsaw and install.

**Within 4 hours of installing the floor,** roll the floor with a 100- to 150-pound floor roller. Wait at least 24 hours before walking on the floor again.

##  How to Install Parquet with a Diagonal Layout

**Establish perpendicular working lines** following step 1 on page 93. Measure 5' from the centerpoint along each working line and make a mark. Snap chalk lines between the 5' marks. Mark the centerpoint of these lines, then snap a chalk line through the marks to create a diagonal reference line.

**Lay out a dry run of tiles along a diagonal line.** Adjust your starting point as necessary. Lay the flooring along the diagonal line using adhesive, following the steps for installing parquet (pages 93 to 95). Make paper templates for tile along walls and in corners. Transfer the template measurements to tiles, and cut to fit.

SPECIAL FLOOR PROJECTS • 95

# Decorative Medallion

If anything is more beautiful under your feet than a newly installed hardwood floor, it's a decorative centerpiece that complements the rest of the surface. Ready-made hardwood medallions, such as the one shown in this project, are relatively easy to install and provide a focal point for the entire room.

### TOOLS & MATERIALS

- Medallion
- Installation jig
- Hammer
- Nails
- Notched trowel
- Router
- Eye and ear protection
- Work gloves
- Pry bar
- Wood putty
- Urethane flooring adhesive

**A medallion made from wood strips and veneers** makes a beautiful design highlight when inset into a wood floor. Many stock and custom designs are available from medallion manufacturers.

## How to Install a Decorative Medallion

**Place the medallion on the floor** where you want it installed. Draw a line around the medallion onto the floor.

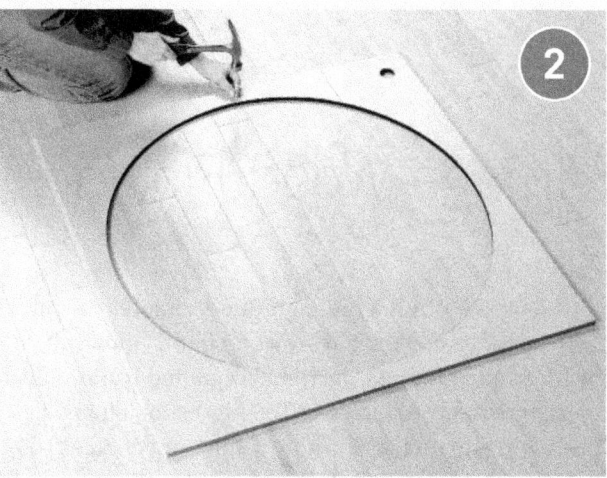

**Nail the installation jig to the floor** so the opening is aligned with the outline you drew in the previous step. Drive the nails into joints in the floor.

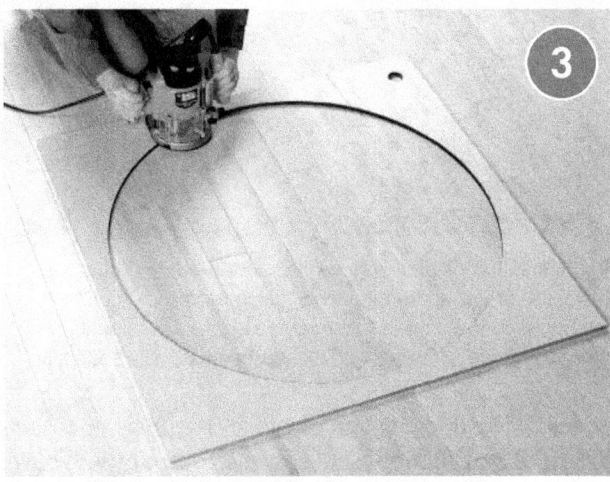

**Using the router bit that came with the medallion,** place the bearing of the router bit on the inside edge of the jig opening and make a ¼"-deep cut. Remove any exposed nails or staples. Make repeated passes with the router, gradually increasing the depth.

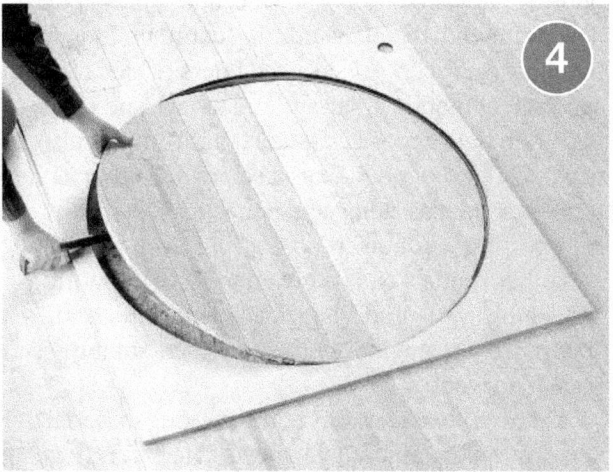

**Use a pry bar** to remove the flooring inside the hole. Remove all nails. Dry-fit the medallion to ensure it fits. Remove the jig and fill nail holes with wood putty.

**Apply urethane flooring adhesive** to the subfloor where the hardwood was removed. Spread the adhesive with a trowel. Set the medallion in place and push it firmly into the adhesive so it's level with the surrounding floor.

SPECIAL FLOOR PROJECTS • 97

# Vintage Wood Floors

**Reclaimed barn siding** was lightly sanded before being installed for the floor in this cozy living room. The color variations in the floor planks provide endless fascination and integrate perfectly with the exposed beams and wood ceiling.

No wood brings a more unique character to your home than a reclaimed wood floor. Once you begin looking for just the right reclaimed wood, you'll inevitably realize that the biggest challenge is narrowing down the amazing number of choices to find the best look for your home.

Old houses and other buildings yield a wealth of wood flooring that can be brought back to life in your home. These include the standard strip flooring harvested from more recent buildings being deconstructed, the plank flooring common to older buildings, more unusual pegged floors (which require special techniques to salvage and re-lay), and even end grain flooring, a tile-type of floor using "bricks" of wood. But older buildings also provide other elements, such as siding and paneling, which can be repurposed as new wood flooring. Even beams and other timbers can be milled to serve as flooring. You simply won't find a larger selection of potential species, styles, and looks for a floor than among reclaimed wood.

There are two ways to get the flooring material you want in the amount you need. The first is to go to the source. Wood flooring is one of the easiest elements to salvage from a building. Removing elements like flooring during deconstruction is called "soft-stripping" for just that reason. Unlike structural members, flooring can be removed with relatively little expertise or effort. Even if you're faced with converting square-cut siding or paneling to your purposes, you can turn it into flooring by milling your own tongue and grooves into the boards. Certainly, this is a lot of work and requires the right tools and attention to detail. But do-it-yourself milling can save you enormous amounts of money.

However, you may simply prefer to go the easier route and purchase reclaimed flooring in quantity from any of a number of salvage firms and companies that deal in reclaimed wood. Consider available stock carefully. Not only do you need to ensure that the amount of a given flooring available through the supplier is sufficient for your needs, you also need to know the flooring you buy is fairly consistent board to board. In most cases, the company will have removed all the boards as part of a single salvage project, so the boards were already fit together as a floor. Sometimes, a bit of mixing and matching does occur. But for the most part, suppliers will have grouped like boards, and many even prefinish the boards, making installation even easier.

Generally, you'll use the same process to install a reclaimed wood floor as you would a new wood floor. However, some techniques may differ, depending on the type of flooring you've chosen. For instance, if you're installing an aged, exceptionally wide plank floor, you may need to facenail—and plug over the facenails—to ensure against cupping or warping. The same is true if you've reclaimed a pegged wood floor and are re-creating that distinctive look in your new home. Complete the installation with the finish of your choice, whether you're leaving the existing surface largely intact, or completely sanding down and refinishing it.

# Reclaiming a Vintage Wood Floor

Reclaiming some wood building materials directly from an existing structure can be a challenge. Structural members such as timbers and beams must be extracted carefully to prevent wholesale collapse. Others, such as siding, are arduous to remove and will need exceptional amounts of prep to be reused. But wood flooring is one of the easiest and most rewarding materials to salvage. Do it right, and you may not even need to refinish the reclaimed flooring after you re-install it.

The process is fairly straightforward and is basically the reverse of installing a wood floor. Start by clearing the room you're working in and remove shoe or other base moldings. Remove the first and possibly second row of boards on the tongue side of the floor. This may require destroying one or more boards to gain access. Do that by using a pry bar on damaged flooring, or a circular saw and pry bar, to cut into and tear out boards so that you have clear access for prying out the adjacent rows.

Removing planks from that point is relatively easy. Slide the tongue of a pry bar under the tongue of the plank next to a nail, and pry the nail up. Do this at each nail location until the plank is completely loose. Then pry up and toward you to release it from the next row. Continue removing planks, taking care not to damage the tongues as you remove the boards. Remove all the nails as you work, and check boards for nails before finally placing them neatly in stacks separated by bolsters.

**Stack reclaimed flooring neatly, well supported by spacers.** If you are planning on using the flooring with its existing finish intact, separate the layers with building paper.

### SALVAGE WISDOM: ACCLIMATING RECLAIMED FLOORS

Wood planks or strips that you reclaim should already be thoroughly dry, because they have likely been inside for decades. However, in some cases you will have rescued the wood from a dilapidated building so far gone that the floors were exposed to the elements for quite a while. In other cases, resellers may have stored reclaimed wood flooring outside. Wood flooring in these situations can absorb moisture. But even if it's just a matter of temperature change, you need to give the flooring a chance to adjust to its new environment. That's why, just as you would with new wood flooring, you should store reclaimed wood planks, strips, or end grain tiles in the room where they will ultimately be installed for at least 24 hours prior to installation.

# How to Mill Tongues and Grooves

### TOOLS & MATERIALS

Reclaimed lumber
Jointer
Tablesaw
Dado blade
Clamps
Scrap wood
Sandpaper
Eye and ear protection
Work gloves

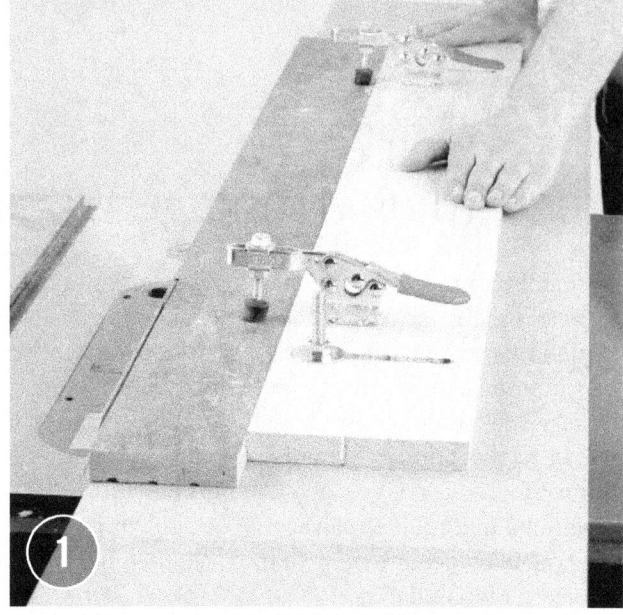

**Joint one edge of each plank using a jointer.** If you don't have a jointer, you can joint the edge using a table saw with a jointer jig. A properly jointed edge will be necessary for the boards to fit snugly together when laid as a floor.

**Use a table saw** to rip the opposite edge of each board so that it is perfectly parallel to the jointed edge.

**Saw the grooves first.** Set a dado blade to the appropriate height, and set the table saw fence so that the groove runs along the middle of the edge. Stack dado blades as necessary to cut wider grooves in thicker stock. Cut the first groove in a test piece.

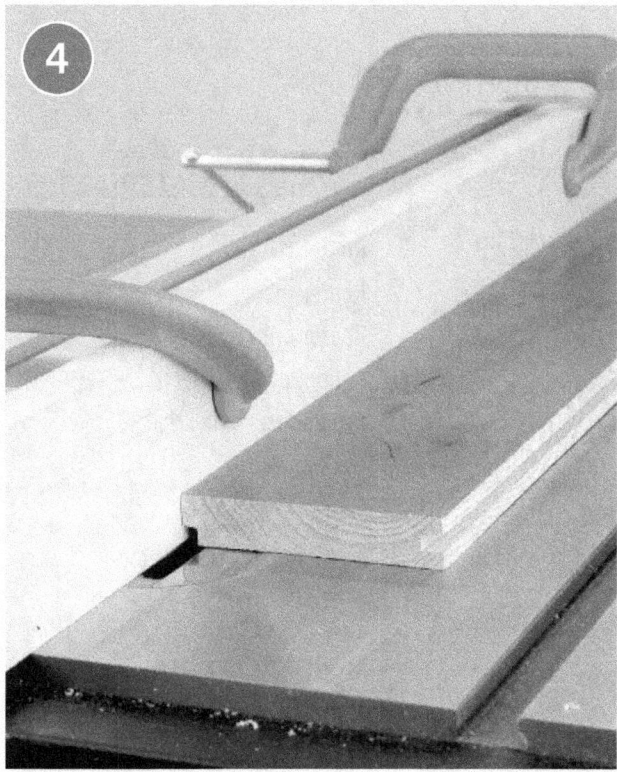

**Reset the fence to cut the tongues.** Use a short or scrap piece to cut the first tongue. Err on the side of cutting tongues too thick, because you can always cut more off, but you'll be in trouble if the tongues do not fit snugly.

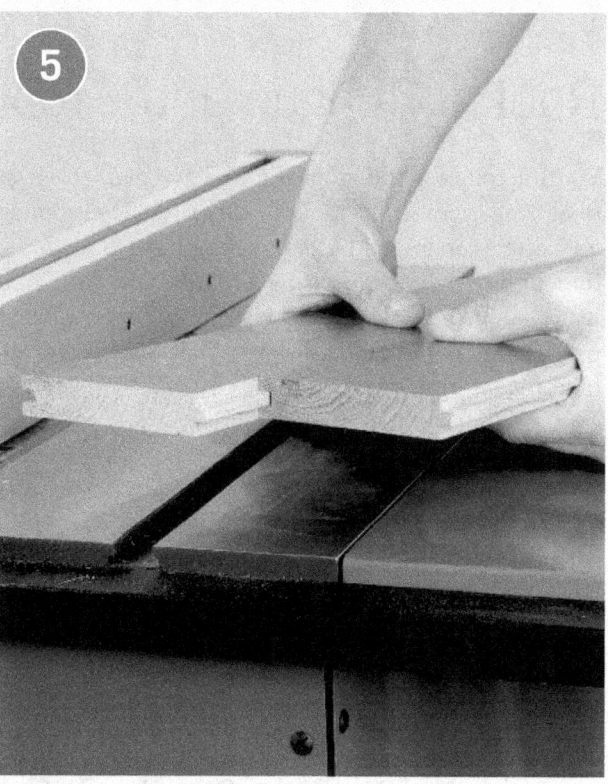

**Check the fit of the tongue into the groove,** with both pieces laying flat. The fit should be snug enough that you have to apply some force to join the two pieces.

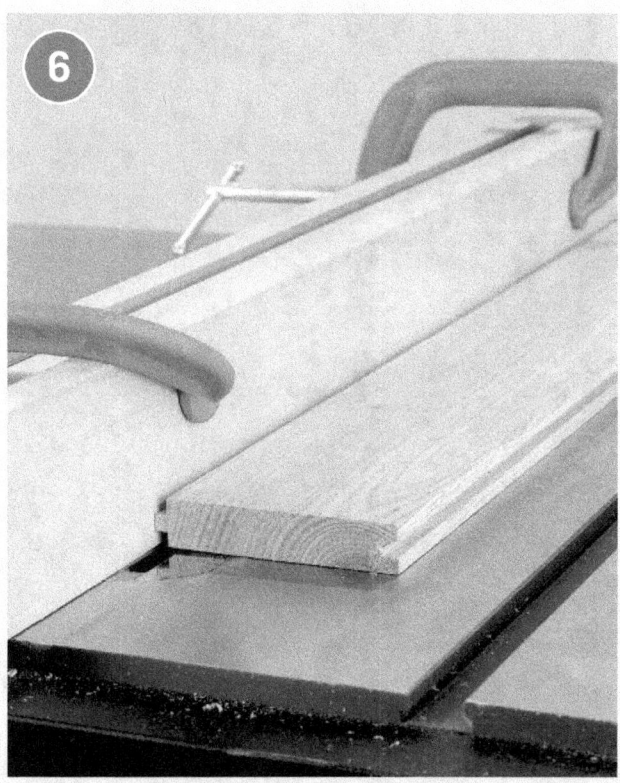

**Once you're certain that the measurements are all correct,** cut all the grooves first. Check each for fit using the tongue on the scrap piece. Finally, cut all the tongues on the other edges of the planks.

**Check all the planks one last time,** paying special attention to any burrs or imperfections in the tongues and grooves. Sand down any spots that might prove troublesome when installing the floor.

SPECIAL FLOOR PROJECTS • 101

# Routing Tongue-and-Groove Flooring

Routing tongues and grooves into wood planks is a great alternative to cutting them with a table saw. The routing is done with special adjustable tongue-and-groove router bits—one for each function. The directions here describe using a router table, although you can also use a hand router with a special jig. The router table, however, is much quicker and easier (and safer) to use. Prepare the planks for routing by jointing and ripping them.

### TOOLS & MATERIALS

Router
Router table
Router bits
Sandpaper
Eye and ear protection
Work gloves

**An adjustable router bit** for cutting tongues.

## How to Rout Tongue-and-Groove Flooring

**Set the groove bit into the router and cut a groove.** Swap the bits and cut a tongue on a sacrificial piece. Check that the tongue and groove fit snugly together, and that the companion pieces sit flat when connected.

**Replace the groove bit and rout all the grooves first.** Swap bits and rout all the tongues. Check that the tongues and grooves are all clean. Sand as necessary to fix any imperfections.

# How to Salvage and Lay Pegged Plank Flooring

 **TOOLS & MATERIALS**

Spade bit
Drill
Wrecker's adze
Hammer
Plug-cutting bit
Pull saw
Chisel
8d finish nails
Glue
Sandpaper
Eye and ear protection
Work gloves

**Remove the first two rows of planks.** Using a spade bit one size smaller than the pegging plugs, drill out the plugs in the face of the boards, exposing the facenails.

**Slip the point of the wrecker's adze** under the edge of the board at the position of one set of facenails. Tap the butt of the adze lightly with a hammer to wedge the adze under the plank. Lever the handle back and forth to loosen the facenails, tapping the adze further under the board as necessary. Continue working the handle until the plank under it can be pulled free without causing damage to the wood.

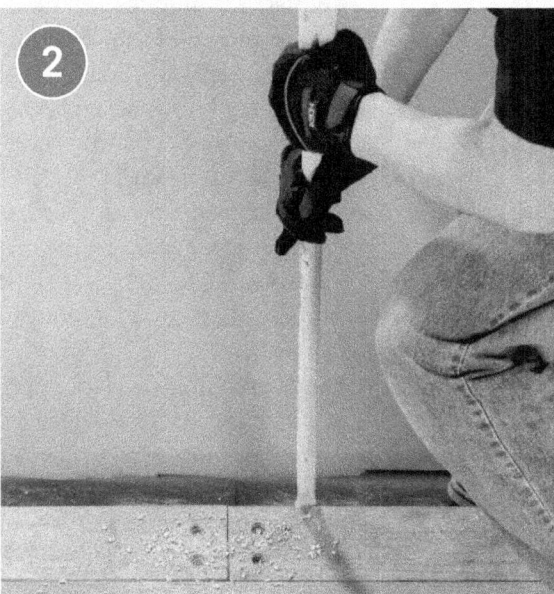

**Lay the flooring** as described in How to Install a Hardwood Plank Floor (pages 67 to 71). Clean out the peg holes with a small chisel, and hammer 8d finish nails through the holes in the face. If you want to add the peg look to plain plank flooring without facenailing, you can also use a spade bit to drill peg holes in the face.

**Once all the planks are installed,** cut the pegs with a drill press fitted with a plug-cutting bit in the correct size. The plugs can be a contrasting wood, or the same wood stained a different finish. Fit the pegs in the holes after coating them with carpenter's glue. Use a pull saw to cut the plug off even with the plank's surface after the glue dries, and sand lightly until smooth.

SPECIAL FLOOR PROJECTS • 103

# End Grain Floors

Spend enough time searching through old industrial buildings and once-grand turn-of-the-century homes, and sooner or later you will come across the interesting and potentially gorgeous wood flooring known as end grain flooring. Also called "wood block" flooring, end grain floors are made of tiles cut from timber ends. Because the cuts are made across the board, the end grain is exposed on the face of the tile, just as it would be on a chopping block. And, as with chopping block, the surface of an end grain tile is incredibly tough and durable.

That durability is why the first uses for these wood block tiles were as a street paving material (and some of those streets are still in existence today) and as floors for industrial facilities. Chances are, you won't find a tougher home flooring material.

But that toughness belies an incredibly beautiful side. End grain pattern is more intense and visually dynamic than any other wood grain. The look of reclaimed end grain tiles varies with the type of wood used and where the tiles were installed. Depending on the look you're after, you can refinish the tiles to create a shiny end grain floor that looks almost like polished brick, or lay a satin-finish surface with hypnotic patterns unlike any other type of flooring. Not only do the tiles present

### END GRAIN TILES: CUT YOUR OWN

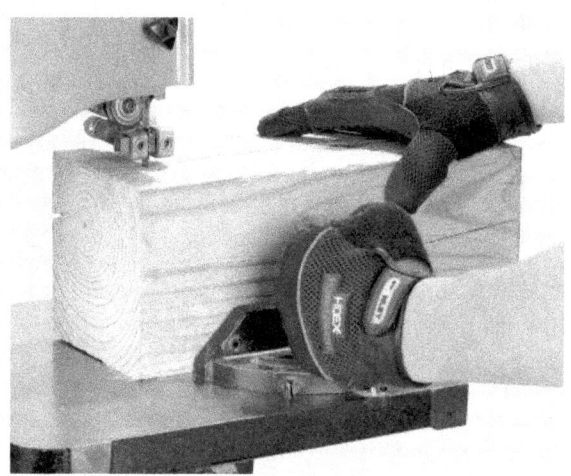

**You can make your own reclaimed end grain tiles** to have a wood block floor. Use a bandsaw to cut inch-thick slices from a 2 × 6 or other piece of reclaimed lumber (such as the antique pine timber being sliced into tiles).

a vast number of potential surface finishes, the arrangement of the tiles can be varied from a simple brick pattern, to a herringbone design, to a more random pattern. You can also leave spaces between the end grain blocks to be filled with flexible wood filler, or you can butt each tile up against the others to create a solid-surface appearance. Either way, the surface must be sealed to prevent dirt and moisture from penetrating.

The floors are laid somewhat like other tile floors, although the adhesive is different; the surface of an end grain floor is either sealed with a clear polyurethane after cleaning and a very light sanding (if you want to keep the aged appearance) or it is sanded in much the same fashion as a hardwood strip floor is, if you're looking for a completely new surface appearance. But given the potential complexity of the floor's pattern and the work required for laying it, end grain floors are usually limited to smaller spaces and those areas that don't require complex adjustments to the pattern to accommodate built-in fixtures. Either way, an end grain floor is more difficult to install than other wood floors, requiring patience and attention to detail. The result, however, is usually well worth your trouble.

### TOOLS & MATERIALS

| | |
|---|---|
| Sketch paper | Lumber |
| Chalk line | Sandable wood filler |
| Measuring tape | Belt sander |
| Polyurethane adhesive | 60-grit sandpaper |
| Trowel | Eye and ear protection |
| Mallet | Dust mask |
| Spacers | Work gloves |
| Bandsaw or jigsaw | |

# How to Lay End Grain Flooring

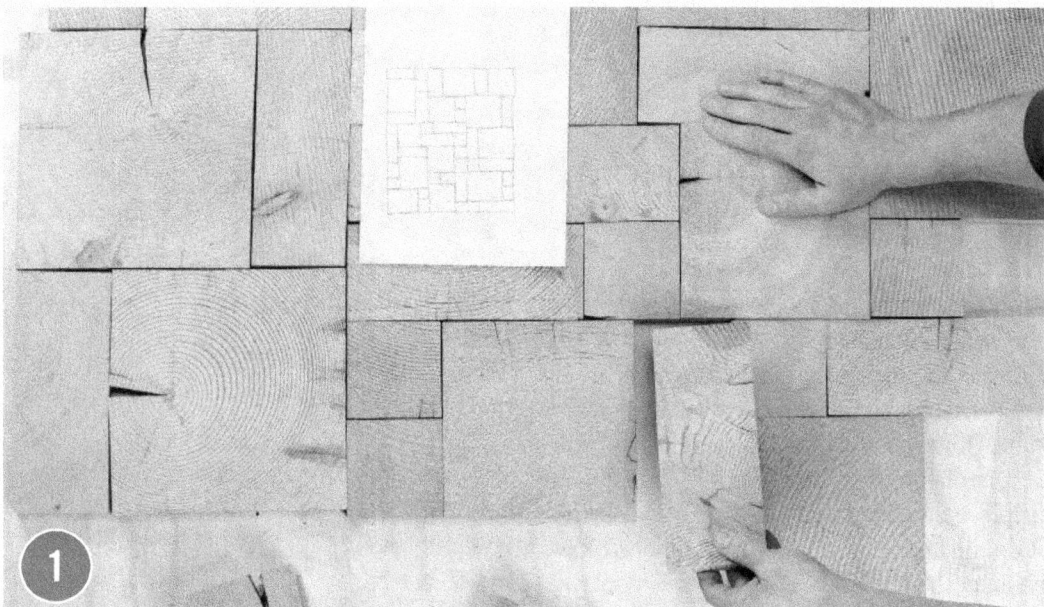

**Establish the overall tile pattern.** Work the pattern out on sketch paper first using the dimensions of the room to scale. Once you've figured out the pattern, dry lay the actual tiles to ensure that it works to your satisfaction.

**Snap chalk lines** to divide the space into four quadrants. Lay one quadrant at a time, starting at the center. Spread a bed of polyurethane adhesive, according to the manufacturer's instructions, setting the tiles in place either butted up to one another, or using spacers to leave room for grout. Tap with a rubber mallet to set into place.

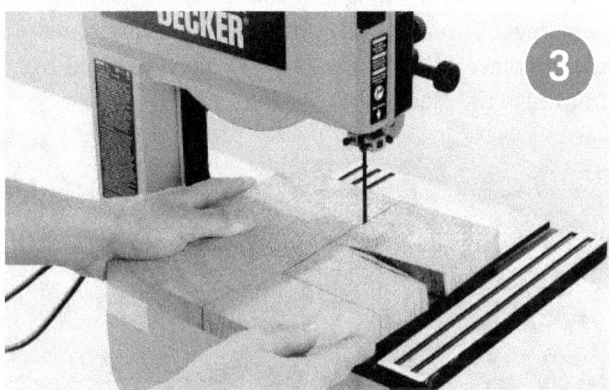

**Cut tiles with a bandsaw or jigsaw** as necessary to fit around obstacles and at the outer edges of the design. Leave a ½" gap at walls and around obstructions such as pillars, to allow for expansion. Once all the tiles are laid, let the floor set for 24 hours, or as long as recommended by the adhesive manufacturer.

**Spread flexible, sandable wood filler** into large cracks in the surface of individual tiles. If you're refinishing the surface, sand with a belt sander equipped with 60-grit sandpaper.

# One-Piece Base Molding

## TOOLS & MATERIALS

Pencil
Tape measure
Power miter saw
T-bevel
Framing square
Sandpaper
Coping saw
Metal file set
Pneumatic finish nail gun & compressor
Moldings
Pneumatic fasteners
Carpenter's glue
Finishing putty
Eye and ear protection
Work gloves

Installing plain, one-piece baseboard such as ranch-style base or cove base is a straightforward project. Outside corner joints are mitered, inside corners are coped, and long runs are joined with scarf cuts.

The biggest difficulty to installing base is dealing with out-of-plumb and nonsquare corners. However, a T-bevel makes these obstacles easy to overcome. Plan the order of your installation prior to cutting any pieces and lay out a specific piece for each length of wall. It may be helpful to mark the type of cut on the back of each piece so you don't have any confusion during the install.

Locate all studs and mark them with painter's tape 6 inches higher than your molding height. If you need to make any scarf joints along a wall, make sure they fall on the center of a stud. Before you begin nailing trim in place, take the time to prefinish the moldings. Doing so will minimize the cleanup afterward.

**Baseboard trim** is installed to conceal the joint between the finished floor and the wallcovering.

# How to Install One-Piece Base Molding

**Measure, cut, and install the first piece of baseboard.** Butt both ends into the corners tightly. For longer lengths, it is a good idea to cut the piece slightly oversized (up to 1/16" on strips over 10' long) and "spring" it into place. Nail the molding in place with two nails at every stud location.

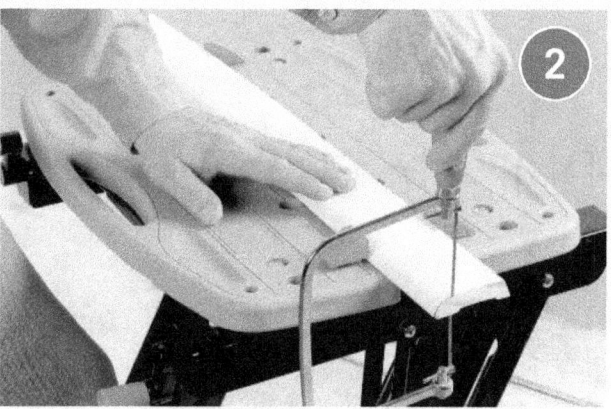

**Cut the second piece of molding oversized by 6" to 10"** and cope-cut the adjoining end to the first piece. Fine-tune the cope with a metal file and sandpaper. Dry fit the joint, adjusting it as necessary to produce a tight-fitting joint.

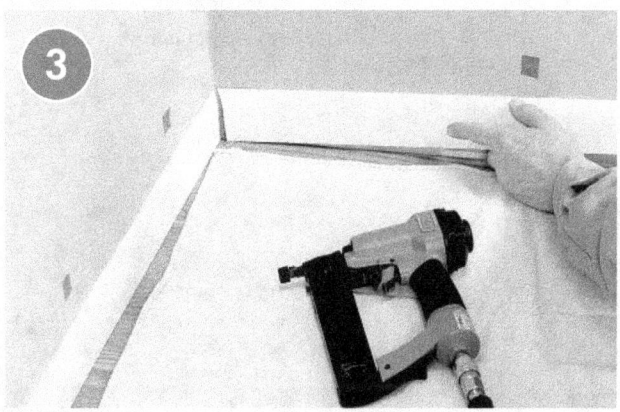

**Check the corner for square with a framing square.** If necessary, adjust the miter cut of your saw. Use a T-bevel to transfer the proper angle. Cut the second piece (coped) to length and install it with two nails at each stud location.

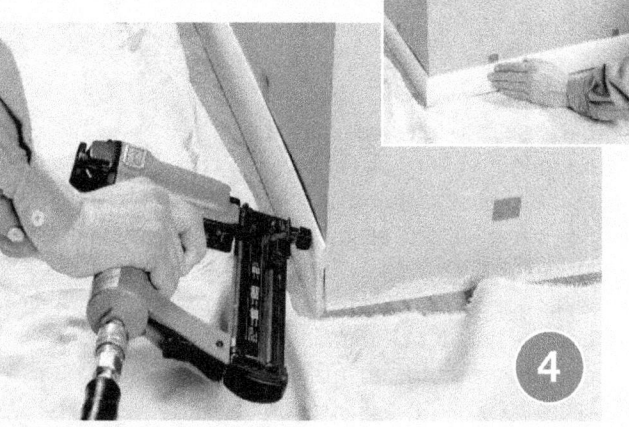

**Adjust the miter angle of your saw** to cut the adjoining outside corner piece. Test-fit the cut to ensure a tight joint (inset photo). Remove the mating piece of trim and fasten the first piece for the outside corner joint.

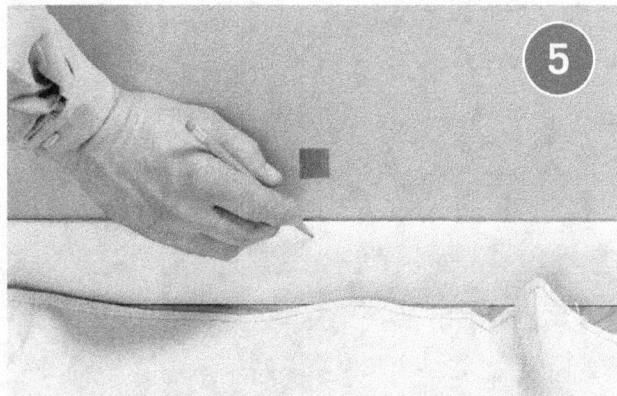

**Lay out any scarf joints** by placing the piece in position so that the previous joint is tight, and then marking the center of a stud location nearest the opposite end. Set the angle of your saw to a 30° angle and cut the molding at the marked location.

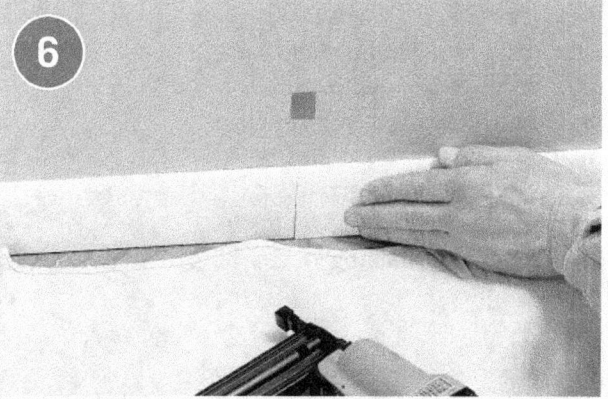

**Nail the third piece in place,** making sure the outside corner joint is tight. Cut the end of the fourth piece to match the scarf joint angle and nail it in place with two nails at each stud location. Add the remaining pieces of molding, fill the nail holes with putty, and apply a final coat of finish.

SPECIAL FLOOR PROJECTS

# Built-Up Base Molding

Built-up base molding is made up of several strips of wood (usually three) that are combined for a particular effect. It is installed in two common scenarios: (1) to match existing trim in other rooms of a house or (2) to match a stock one-piece molding that is not available.

Installing a built-up base molding is no more difficult than a standard one-piece molding, because the same installation techniques are used. However, built-up base molding offers a few advantages over standard stock moldings. Wavy floors and walls are easier to conceal, and the height of the molding is completely up to you, making heat registers and other obstructions easier to deal with.

In this project, the base molding is made of high-grade plywood rather than solid 1× stock lumber. Plywood is more economical and dimensionally stable than solid lumber and can be built up to any depth, as well as cut down to any height. Keep in mind that plywood molding is less durable than solid wood and is only available in 8- and 10-foot lengths, making joints more frequent.

### TOOLS & MATERIALS

- Pneumatic finish nail gun
- Air compressor
- Air hose
- Miter saw
- Hammer
- Nail set
- Pencil
- Tablesaw or straight-edge guide and circular saw
- Tape measure
- Sandpaper
- Power sander
- ¾" finish-grade oak plywood
- Brad nailer
- ⅝, 1¼" brad nails
- Base shoe molding
- Cap molding
- 2" finish nails
- Wood putty
- Wood glue
- Eye and ear protection
- Work gloves

**If you can't find your exact trim molding at a local lumberyard,** try recreating it with multiple pieces. High-grade plywood can be substituted for the solid baseboard shown here.

# How to Install Built-Up Base Molding

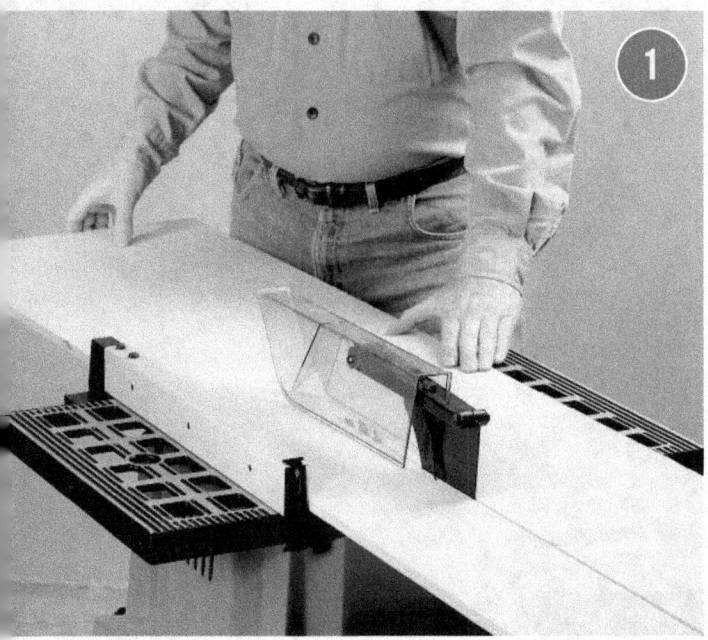

**Cut the plywood panel into 6" strips** with a tablesaw or a straightedge guide and a circular saw. Lightly sand the strips, removing any splinters left from the saw. Then apply the finish of your choice to the moldings and the plywood strips. Install the plywood strips with 2" finish nails driven at stud locations. Use scarf joints on continuous runs, driving pairs of fasteners into the joints. Cut and install moldings so that all scarf joints fall at stud locations.

**Test-fit inside corner butt joints** before cutting a workpiece. If the walls are not square or straight, angle or bevel the end cut a few degrees to fit the profile of the adjoining piece. The cap molding will cover any gaps at the top of the joint.

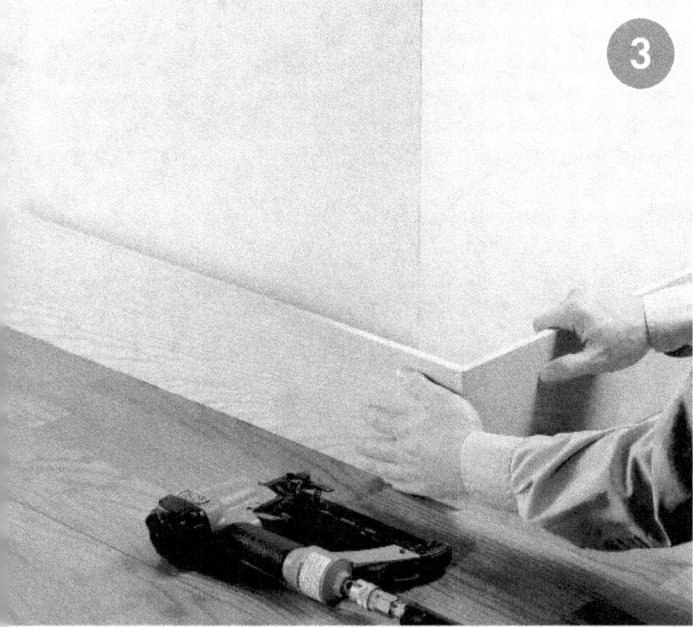

**Miter outside corners squarely at 45°.** Use wood glue and 1¼" brad nails to pull the mitered pieces tight, and then nail the base to the wall at stud locations with 2" finish nails. Small gaps at the bottom or top of the base molding will be covered with cap or base shoe.

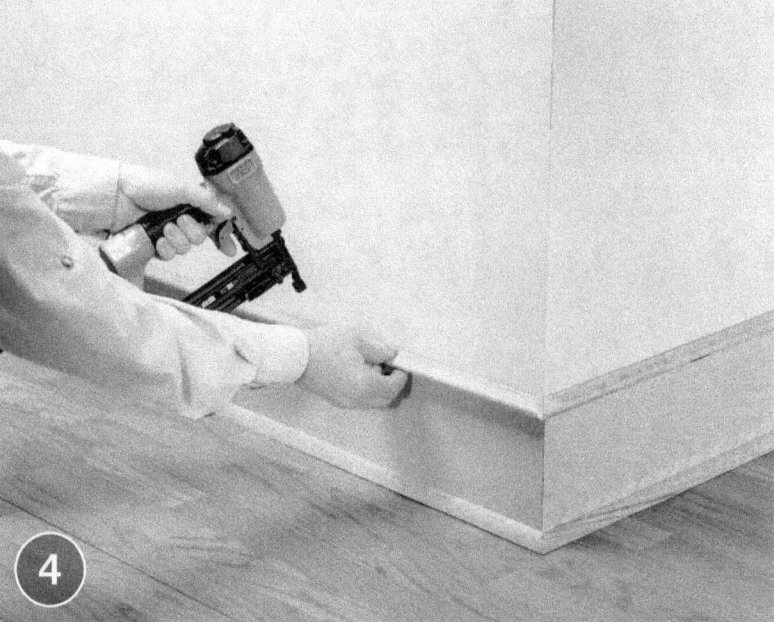

**Use a brad nailer with 18-gauge,** ⅝" brads to install the cap and base shoe moldings along the edges of the plywood base. Fit scarf joints on longer lengths, coped joints on inside corners, and miter joints on outside corners. Stagger the seams so that they do not line up with the base molding seams. Set any protruding nails with a nail set and fill all nail holes with putty.

# FINISH & MAINTAIN WOOD FLOORS

Wood floors do show their wear eventually, and occasionally surface damage will mar their beauty. Sometimes boards loosen and a squeak develops. It's good to know exactly how to maintain your wood and laminate floors in the short term and how to repair them in the long term.

Finishing Wood Floors covers applying various finishes to bare wood floors. Some variations of wood stains and how to apply them are shown in addition to some techniques to create an aged- or distressed-looking finish. You will learn application techniques for the old-time but newly trendy wax finishes.

Many people don't realize that wood floors can be painted, and in fact painted floors were very popular in the eighteen hundreds. Painting is a great solution for a wood floor that has lost its luster but cannot be sanded down to bare wood.

Maintaining Wood Floors gets into the maintenance and repair of wood floors. Should you ever need to remove a stain of any sort from your wood floor, this section has all the answers for getting the best results from stain removers. Should your stain removal be unsuccessful, or should more serious damage occur to your floor, this section also shows in detail how to refinish a wood floor or replace damaged floorboards and laminate. Instructions on replacing a damaged stair tread are also included.

# Finishing Wood Floors

One of the most desirable features of hardwood flooring is that it's a natural product, with grain patterns that are interesting to the eye and a combination of colors that gives any room a soft, inviting glow. The resilience of wood fibers makes a hardwood floor extremely durable, but they are susceptible to changes caused by moisture and aging.

Typically, the first thing to wear out on a hardwood floor is the finish. Refinishing the floor by sanding it with a rented drum sander and applying a top coat, such as polyurethane, will make your old floor look new. If you want to retain the floor's aged glow without sanding, or if the boards have been sanded before and are less than ⅜ inches thick, consider stripping the floor.

Once your floor is finished, you may want to dress it up with a favorite design, border, or pattern. If the wood will not look good refinished, consider painting it. Pages 120 to 123 offer exciting ways to customize your wood floor.

### In this chapter:
- Floor Stains & Finishes
- Wax Finishes
- Painting Wood Floors

# Floor Stains & Finishes

A stain is applied to the surface of an unfinished wood floor to change the color to a variety of natural wood tones. Colored stains can also be applied to previously stained and finished floors for a colorwashed effect. Consider a colored stain to complement your décor; green blends well with a rustic decorating scheme and white adds to a contemporary look.

Look for a water-based stain that's formulated for easy application without lap marks or streaking. Conditioners can help prevent streaking and control grain raise when you're using water-based wood stains. Use a wood conditioner on the wood prior to staining, if recommended by the manufacturer.

You can also stain wood by colorwashing it with diluted latex paint. The colorwash solution will be considerably lighter in color than the original paint color. Use one part latex paint and four parts water to make a colorwash solution, and experiment with small amounts of paint until you achieve the desired color. Apply the stain or colorwash solution in an inconspicuous area, such as a closet, to test the application method and color before staining the entire floor surface.

Aged finishes (page 117) give floors timeworn character, which is especially suitable for a rustic or transitional decorating style. Although they appear distressed and fragile, these finishes are very durable. Aged finishes are especially suitable on previously painted or stained floors, but they may also be applied to new or resurfaced wood flooring. Up to three coats of paint in different colors may be used.

## TOOLS & MATERIALS

- Synthetic brush
- Sponge applicators
- Rubber gloves
- Paint pad and pole extension
- Power sander
- Vacuum
- Fine- and medium-grit sandpaper
- Tack cloth
- Water-based stain or latex paint
- High-gloss and satin clear finishes
- Lint-free rags
- Latex enamel paints
- Paint roller
- Hammer
- Chisel
- Awl
- Eye and ear protection

# Wood Stain Variations

**Dark wood tones** work well for traditional rooms. White colorwashing over a previously dark-stained floor mellows the formal appearance.

**Medium, warm wood tones** have a casual appearance. White colorwashing over a medium wood tone results in an antiqued look.

**Pale neutral stains** are often used for contemporary rooms. A blue colorwash can give a pale floor bold new character.

# How to Apply Stain to a Bare Wood Floor

**Sand the floor surface** with fine-grit sandpaper in the direction of the wood grain. Remove the sanding dust with a vacuum, then wipe the floor with a tack cloth.

**Prepare and apply stain.** Wear rubber gloves when working with any stain product. Stir the stain or colorwash solution thoroughly. Apply the stain or solution to the floor using a synthetic brush or sponge applicator. Work on one small section at a time. Keep a wet edge and avoid overlapping the brush strokes.

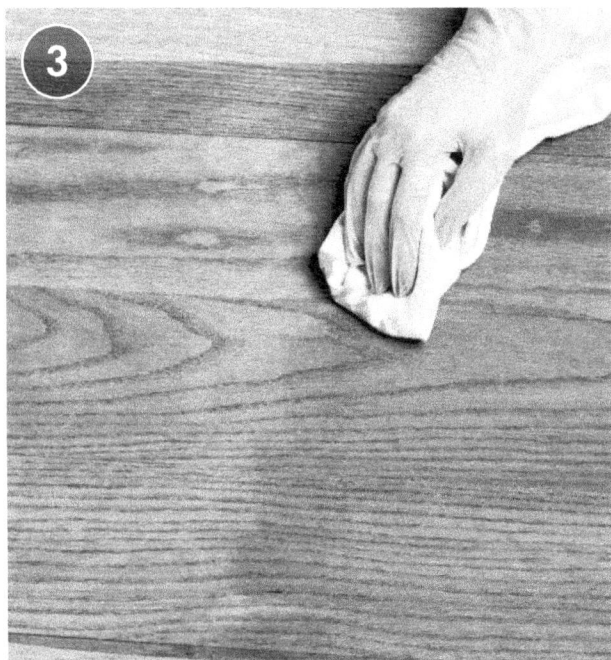

**Wipe away excess stain after the waiting time** recommended by the manufacturer using a dry, lint-free rag. Wipe across the grain of the wood first, then wipe with the grain. Continue applying and wiping stain until the entire floor is finished. Allow the stain to dry. Sand the floor lightly using fine-grit sandpaper, then remove any sanding dust with a tack cloth. For a deeper color, apply a second coat of stain and allow it to dry thoroughly.

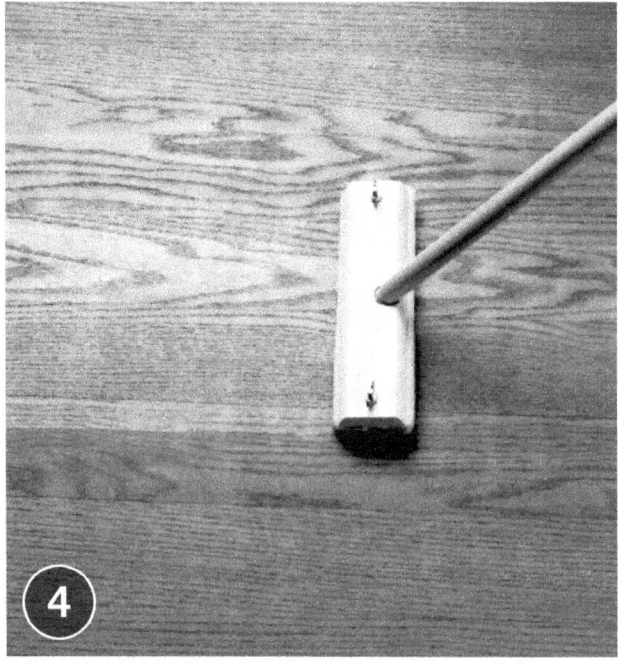

**Apply a coat of high-gloss clear finish to the stained floor** using a sponge applicator or a paint pad with pole extension. Allow the finish to dry. Sand the floor lightly using fine-grit sandpaper, then wipe with a tack cloth. Apply two coats of satin clear finish following manufacturer's directions.

## How to Apply an Aged & Distressed Finish

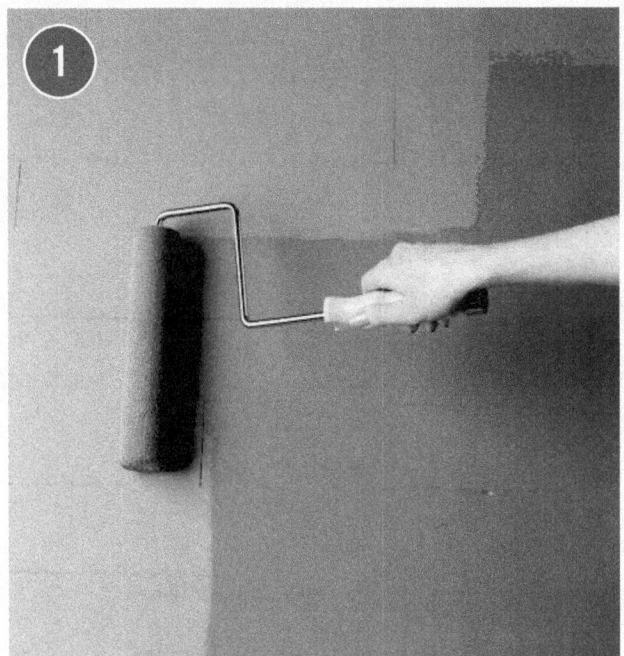

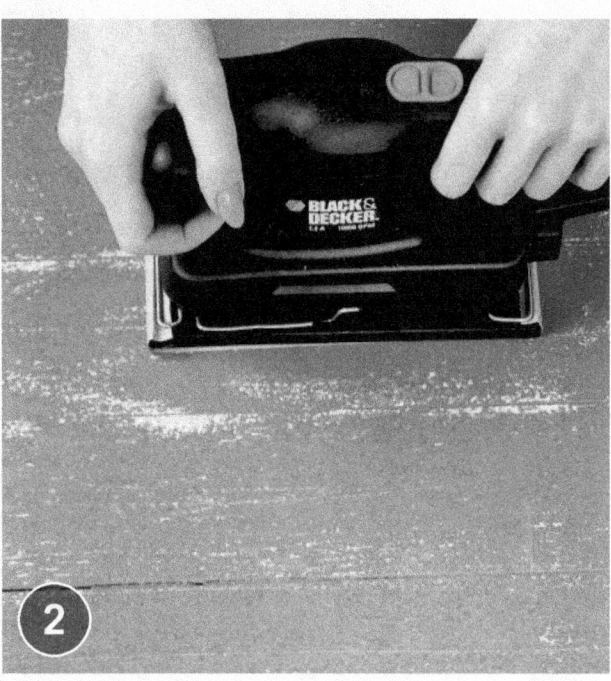

**Finish the floor with a painted or stained base coat.** Sand the floor lightly using fine-grit sandpaper. Vacuum the floor and wipe away dust with a tack cloth. Apply two or three coats of enamel using a different color of paint for each coat. Allow the floor to dry between coats. Sand the floor lightly between coats using fine-grit sandpaper, and wipe away dust with a tack cloth.

**Use a power sander to sand the floor surface** with medium grit sandpaper, sanding harder in some areas to remove the top and middle coats of paint. Avoid sanding beyond the base coat of paint or stain.

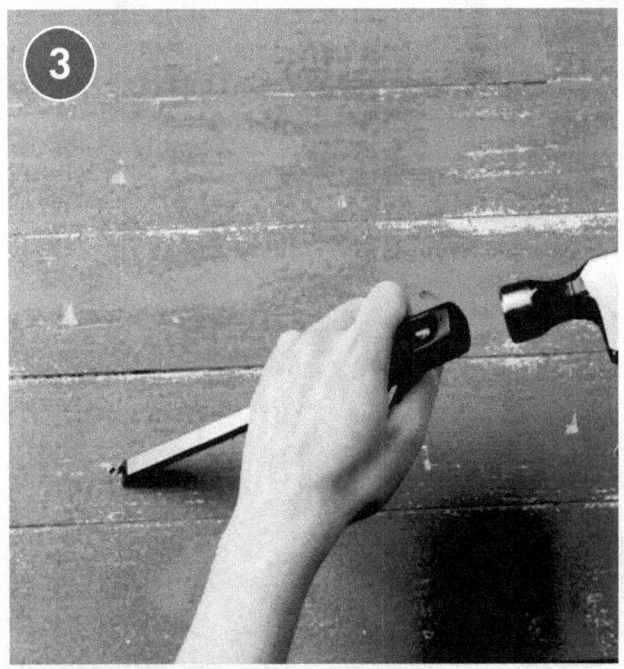

 ### CREATIVE COLOR OPTIONS

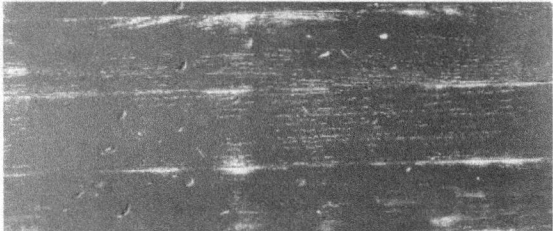

**Two coats of dark green paint** were applied over a previously stained floor. Sanding revealed the stain in some areas. The floor was further distressed using a hammer, chisel, and awl.

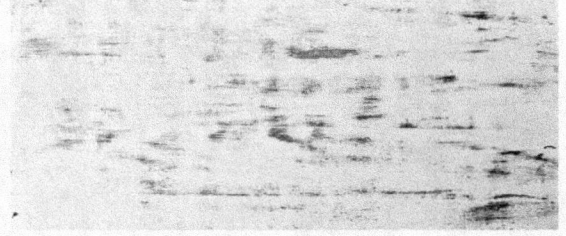

**Maroon base coat and light rose top coat** were painted over a previously stained floor. Sanding created an aged look suitable for a cottage bedroom.

**To distress the floor further,** hit the wood with the head of a hammer or a chain. Gouge the boards with a chisel, or pound holes randomly using an awl. Create as many imperfections as desired, then sand the floor lightly with fine-grit sandpaper. Apply two coats of satin clear finish, allowing the floor to dry completely between coats.

# Wax Finishes

The new trend in floor finishing is the old standard of wax. Your ancestors might not understand why anyone wouldn't choose polyurethane, or better yet, a factory finished floor, but there are some plusses to wax. The first benefit is that the sheen on a waxed floor can be changed by simply changing the style pad used to buff the floor. The lower sheen possible with waxes is appealing when used with the new hand-scraped boards. Another benefit with wax is that removing the finish does not remove any of the wood, as sanding would for a typical polyurethane finish. A typical homeowner can easily touch up areas with a rental buffer. Some products combine oil and wax, such as Pallmann Magic Oil.

Wax needs to be applied to bare, unfinished wood floors. Pay careful attention to the manufacturer's instructions on the application method and type of pads used for the buffer.

### TOOLS & MATERIALS

Vacuum
Wax finish
Buffer with red or tan pad and white pad
Cheesecloth
Eye and ear protection
Rubber gloves

**Wax can have beautiful results** when applied to an unfinished hardwood floor.

# How to Apply Wax Finish

**1**

**Apply wax using cheesecloth.** Vacuum the floor thoroughly. Wrap a generous amount of wax in cheesecloth and apply to the floor in a circular pattern.

**2**

**Buffing is the final step in wax application.** Check product directions for the type of pad.

# Painting Wood Floors

Paint is a quick, cost-effective way to cover up wood floors that no longer look their best, but a floor doesn't have to be distressed or damaged to benefit from paint. Floors in perfect condition in both formal and informal spaces can be decorated with paint to add color and personality. For example, one could unify a space by extending a painted floor through a hallway to a staircase. Stencil designs or faux finishes can make an oversized room feel cozy and inviting. There are even techniques for disguising worn spots. In addition, paint is a relatively inexpensive flooring finish if your budget is tight.

### TOOLS & MATERIALS

- Lacquer thinner
- Primer
- Latex paint specifically for floors
- Wide painter's tape
- Tape measure
- Paint roller and tray
- 4"-wide paintbrush
- Extension pole
- Paint scraper
- Hammer
- Pole sander
- Putty knife
- Nail set
- Dust mask
- Fine- and medium-grit sandpaper
- Broom
- Vacuum
- Tack cloth
- Stir sticks
- Paint can opener
- Polyurethane sealer
- Paint pad
- Straightedge
- Eye and ear protection
- Rubber gloves
- Work gloves

**Rev up a worn-out floor with a bright paint color.** Paint not only disguises flaws, but can also add warmth and character to a room.

# How to Paint Wood Floors

**To paint a wood floor you must apply primer first,** then apply the paint, and follow that with a polyurethane sealer. Make sure the products you choose are made specifically for floors.

**Use a paint scraper to smooth rough spots.** Use a pole sander to sand with the grain of the wood. For coarse wood, use medium-grit sandpaper. Scuff glossy hardwoods with fine sandpaper (120-grit) for good adhesion.

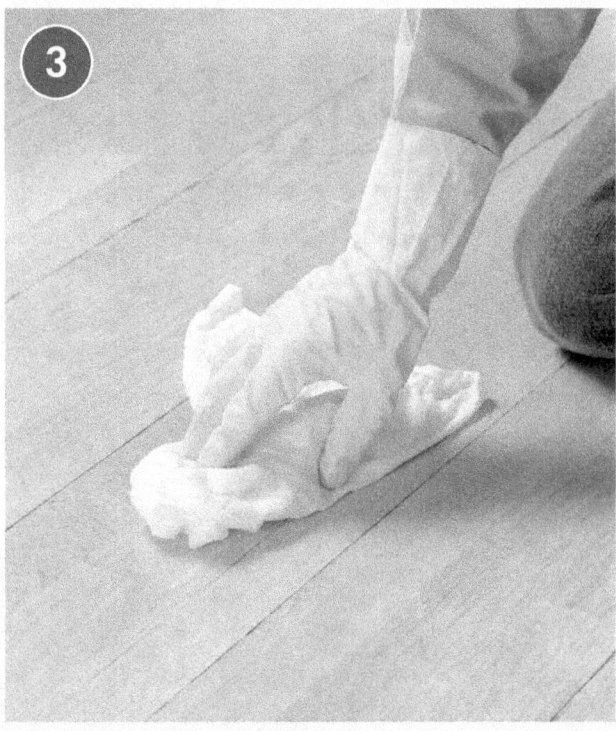

**Clean up dust with a broom or vacuum.** Use a damp cloth to remove fine dust. Use a cloth dampened with lacquer thinner for a final cleaning. If you see any nails sticking up, tap them down with a hammer and nail set.

**Protect the baseboards with wide painter's tape.** Press the tape edges down so paint doesn't seep underneath.

*(continued)*

**Mix primer well** (see step 6 for mixing technique). Use a 4"-wide brush to apply the primer around the perimeter of the room. Then paint the remaining floor with a roller on an extension pole. Allow the primer to dry.

**To mix paint,** pour half of the paint into another can, stirring the paint in both containers with a wooden stir stick before recombining them. As you stir, you want a smooth consistency.

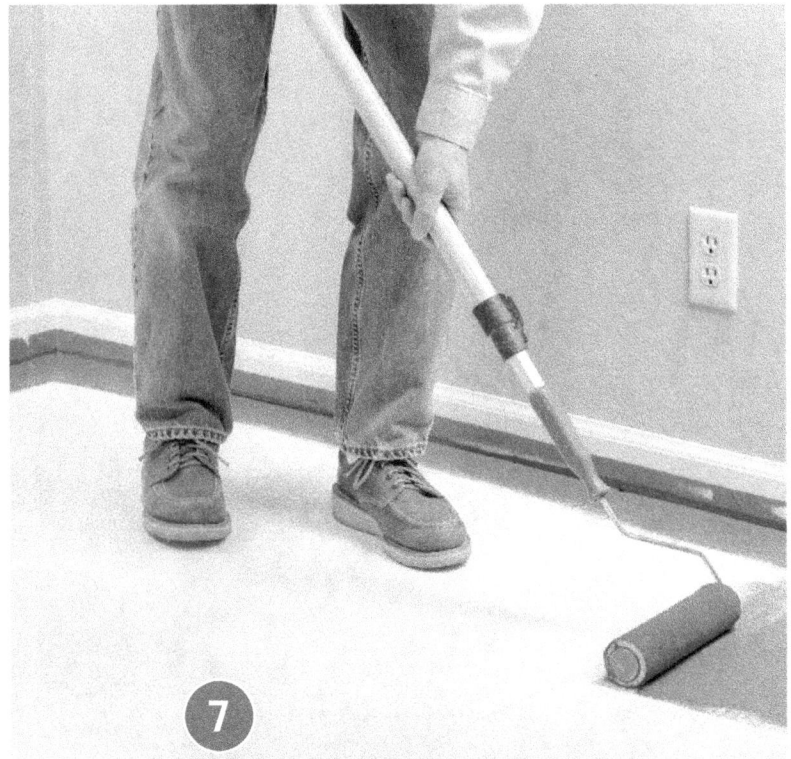

**Use a 4" brush** to apply paint around the border. To paint the rest of the floor, use a roller on an extension pole. Always roll from a dry area to a wet area to minimize lap lines. Allow paint to dry. Apply second coat of paint. Allow to dry.

**Apply 2 or 3 coats of a matte-finish,** waterbased polyurethane sealer using a painting pad on a pole. Allow the paint to dry. Sand with a pole sander using fine sandpaper. Clean up dust with a tack cloth.

# How to Paint a Checkerboard Floor

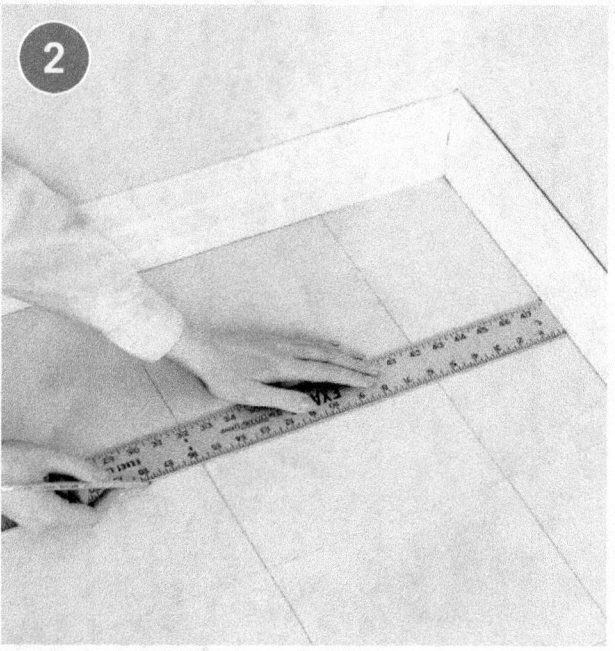

**If your wood floor is in poor condition,** it can be camouflaged with a design, such as a classic checkerboard pattern. Proper preparation is essential for lasting results. If you've already painted the floor based on the instructions from the first half of this project, you are well on your way, and you have the base color already painted. You just have to paint in the darker-colored squares.

**Measure the entire floor.** Now, determine the size of squares you'll use. Plan the design so the areas of the floor with the highest visibility, such as the main entrance, have full squares. Place partial squares along the walls in less conspicuous areas. Mark the design lines on the floor using a straightedge and pencil.

**Using painter's tape,** outline the squares that are to remain light in color. Press firmly along all edges of the tape using a putty knife to create a tight seal.

**Paint the remaining squares with the darker paint color.** Paint small areas at a time. Once you have painted the entire box and a few surrounding boxes, remove the masking tape from the painted squares. Be sure to remove the tape before the paint completely dries. After all of the paint has completely dried, apply a coat of high-gloss clear finish using a paint roller or paint pad with a pole extension. Allow the finish to dry.

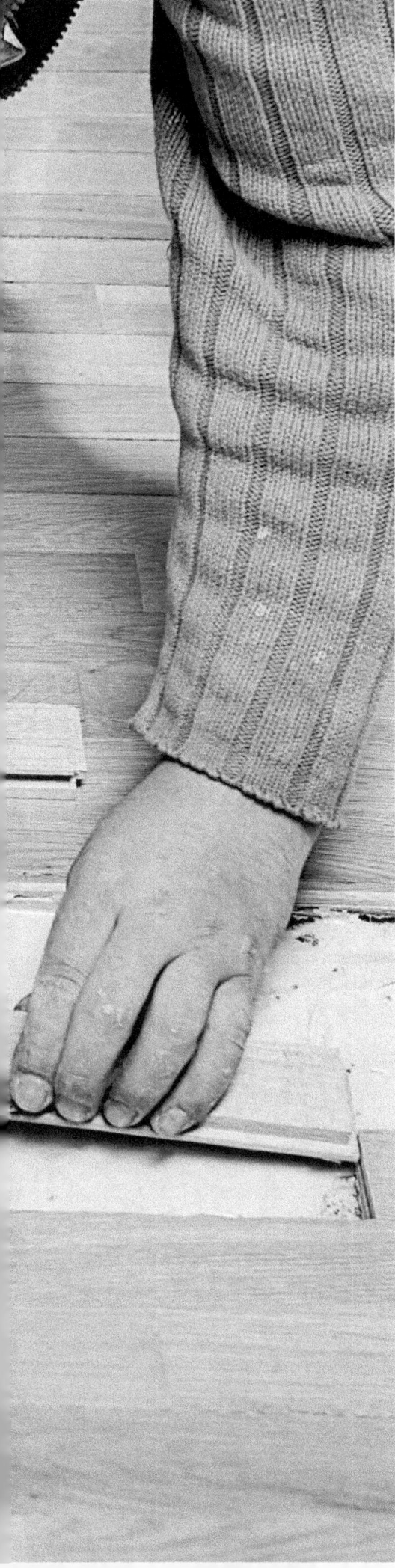

# Maintaining Wood Floors

Wood floors are among the most durable flooring materials you can install, but like any flooring, they require occasional maintenance to preserve their look and function. Years of regular, normal use can wear out the surface finishes, and even the hardest woods can be scratched by pets with sharp toenails or by furniture dragged along their surface. Impact by heavy items—tools or even heavy dishes—can dent a wood floor. And the biggest enemy of all is water, which can badly stain wood, or even warp it to the point where your only option is complete replacement.

This chapter will show you the tried-and-true basics of cleaning and maintaining wood floors to provide years of service, as well as solutions to the most common problems with wood floors.

The best strategies for caring for wood floors are the classic methods practiced by wood flooring professionals. Manufacturers market a great many chemical products that proclaim they can strip, restore, and top-coat a floor all in one pass, no matter what your finish might be. Be very wary of these products, as one of the worst things you can do for your fine wood floor is blanket it with additional layers of finishes that do not address underlying problems, and which may not even be compatible with the original finish.

### In this chapter:
- Cleaning & Maintaining a Wood Floor
- Removing Stains from Wood
- Refinishing Hardwood Floors
- Repairing Scratches & Dents to Hardwood Floors
- Fixing Loose & Squeaky Floorboards
- Replacing Damaged Floorboards
- Replacing a Damaged Stair Tread

# Cleaning & Maintaining a Wood Floor

You might think that cleaning a floor needs no explanation—after all, isn't it just a matter of a mop and a bucket?

In some cases, yes, cleaning the floor is that simple, but with wood floors it is important to evaluate the floor carefully before charging in. The type of finish and its condition is critical in choosing the right type of cleaning products and methods.

While hardwood floors installed or refinished in the last 30 years likely have some kind of polyurethane or varnish finish that will be relatively easy to clean, older floors may be finished with shellac, lacquer, or oil finish—all likely covered over with many layers of wax. These floors require different cleaning strategies.

Manufacturers offer a wide variety of products, many of which proclaim that they can be used on any type of floor, no matter what the finish and no matter what the condition of the floor. This is deceiving marketing, because not all surface finishes are compatible with one another. Whenever possible, if you want to apply a fresh top coat, it should match the original finish. It can be especially problematic to apply modern water-based varnishes or polyurethanes over the top of solvent-based shellacs or oils.

And it is almost always disastrous to slather on a new top coat over floors that have been waxed. Even attempts to strip the wax before applying a top coat will rarely get all wax removed. Your only real option with a waxed floor is to clean and rewax it. Floors with a heavy buildup of waxes and top coats will eventually require complete sanding down to bare wood and refinishing with polyurethane.

Remember that virtually all older shellac, lacquer, or oiled floors have multiple layers of wax over them. Treat these floors as wax-finished floors for purposes of cleaning.

Remember that the fallback position for any wood floor that has just too much old wax or finish, or which is too badly damaged, is a complete sanding and refinishing (pages 131 to 132).

## TOOLS & MATERIALS

Polyurethane
Water-based cleaner
Screening and recoating with same polyurethane product
Paste wax
Deep sanding and refinishing with polyurethane; new paste wax; buffing

Acrylic wax
Ammonia-based wax stripper; new acrylic wax
Varnish
Shellac
New polyurethane or deep sanding and refinishing

New shellac or deep sanding and refinishing with Tung oil
Odorless mineral spirits; new oil
Extra-fine steel wool
Rubber gloves

# How to Evaluate & Clean Wood Floors

**Begin by sweeping, vacuuming, then removing dust from the floor** using a pad-mop equipped with wet pad. Scuff marks can be lightly scrubbed by hand using a soft cloth, not an abrasive pad.

**Test the soundness of the finish** by placing a few drops of water on one of the more well-worn spots in the floor. If the water beads remain on the surface of the wood for a few minutes without soaking in, the finish is sound. This will mean that water-based cleaners can be safely used to clean the floor. Use a pH-neutral wood wash to clean the floor and a damp rag to then rinse it.

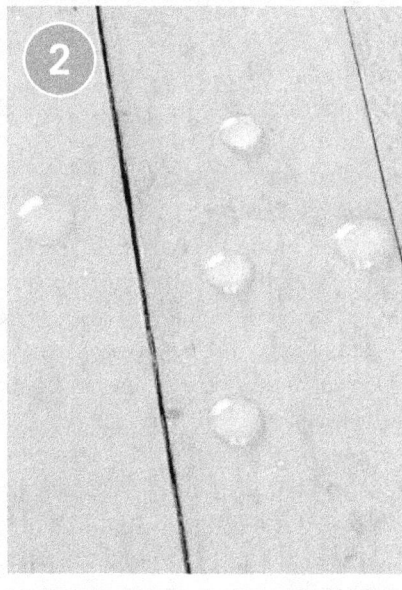

**If the floor finish is not sound,** water will soak into the wood immediately. Do not clean with a water-based product, because it will stain and damage the floor. Instead, clean the floor with cloths dampened with mineral spirits. An unsound floor finish will eventually need to be either recoated with the same finish currently on the floor, or rewaxed. The best long-term solution will be to completely sand and finish with a new polyurethane layer (see pages 131 to 132).

**Next, test to see if your floors have a paste wax finish.** Slightly dampen a piece of extra-fine steel wool and rub the floor in several areas. Paste wax will show up by leaving a gray smudge on the steel wool pad. On a paste-wax floor, clean the floor with cloths moistened with odorless mineral spirits. Let dry completely, then apply a new coating of paste wax, and buff it thoroughly, following manufacturer's directions.

**NOTE:** NEVER apply a water-based finish coat over a waxed floor.

**Does your floor have an acrylic wax?** These newer waxes are best identified by the dirty, patch-like appearance they have as they begin to wear. If your floor has this kind of synthetic wax, use an ammonia-based wax stripper to remove the wax layer, then apply a new layer of acrylic wax. Be aware that acrylic waxes will need frequent reapplication.

# Removing Stains from Wood

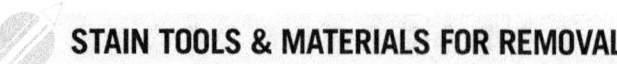

## STAIN TOOLS & MATERIALS FOR REMOVAL

| Stain | Tools & Materials |
|---|---|
| Paint | Paint scraper, abrasive pad, Goof Off |
| Crayon, black heel marks | Mineral spirits |
| Gum | Chill and chip off; mineral spirits |
| Fingernail polish | Lacquer thinner |
| Glue | Water-based household cleaner, or Goof Off. |
| Construction adhesive | Steam and putty knife |
| Coffee, tea | Apple cider vinegar and water |
| Ink | Baking soda and water. |
| Water, iron rust | Oxalic acid and water |
| Grape juice, dye, blood | Chlorine bleach and water |
| Urine, feces | Hydrogen peroxide and sodium hydroxide (27%) |

A variety of substances can stain wood floors, and each substance has a particular solution most likely to produce results. Many stains are surface discolorations that may be able to be removed with nothing more than a light scraping or rubbing with an abrasive pad or fine sandpaper. Always try this before reaching for more serious solutions, some of which require the use of dangerous chemicals.

Some stains, though—especially water stains or stains from pet urine—may soak in very deep and are difficult or impossible to fully remove. In these instances, you should consider replacing entire floorboards (page 144). Another solution is to use a bleach to lighten the color of the stain. Be aware, though, that bleach does not remove a stain, but just lightens it. After bleaching, you will likely be left with the task of restaining the bleached area to match the surrounding floor.

**Paint.** Obvious drips can often be scraped off with a sharp paint scraper. More imbedded paint stains may be amenable to light sanding with a scrub pad or fine sandpaper. A commercial removal product, such as Goof Off, may also work well.

If the floor finish is marred after removal, lightly coating the stain area with polyurethane or another finish may hide it.

**Crayon, black heel marks.** Try a water-based cleaner first, then a cloth lightly dampened with mineral spirits.

**Gum.** Chill with ice and chip off; or try mineral spirits.

**Fingernail polish.** Moisten a cloth with lacquer thinner, and carefully dab the stain. Avoid getting it on the rest of the finish, as it will likely dissolve it. After removal, you may have to touch up the finish.

**Glue.** Most wood glues or household glues are water-based. Begin by trying to simply scrape away the glue. Next, try a water-based cleaner. Last resort: a chemical removal product, like Goof Off.

**Construction adhesive.** Chip away as much as you can, then apply steam with a household iron, and try to scrape away as much as possible. Remaining adhesive may need to be sanded away.

**Coffee and tea.** Dilute ¼ cup of apple cider vinegar in a gallon of water and use a sponge to moisten the stain. Let it sit for 1 to 2 hours, then scrub with a clean sponge. Rinse with a damp sponge and dry immediately.

**Ink.** Mix baking soda and water to form a paste. Spread the paste over the stain. Let sit for a few minutes, then blot up the paste with a damp cloth. Repeat the process until the ink stain is removed.

**Water, iron rust stains.** Mix a solution of oxalic acid and water, following label directions. Apply the solution carefully to the stain and wait several hours, or overnight. Thoroughly wash away the residue with water mixed with baking soda, which neutralizes the acid. Oxalic acid is caustic, so make sure to wear protective gloves and avoid getting it on your skin. This solution will lighten the wood, and you may need to sand and restain the area to match the surrounding floor.

**Grape juice, dye, blood.** Apply household bleach to the stain and blot it up. If it does not remove the stain immediately, reapply and let sit overnight. Neutralize the bleached area with vinegar, then rinse with clear water. If the bleach has removed too much wood color, restain the area to match surrounding wood.

**Urine, feces.** Use a product like Klean Strip, which is a mixture of hydrogen peroxide and sodium hydroxide. This is very caustic and toxic material, so handle carefully. Apply the bleach, and let stand as directed. Rinse with clear water. This product will bleach the wood quite light, so staining and refinishing the area will be necessary.

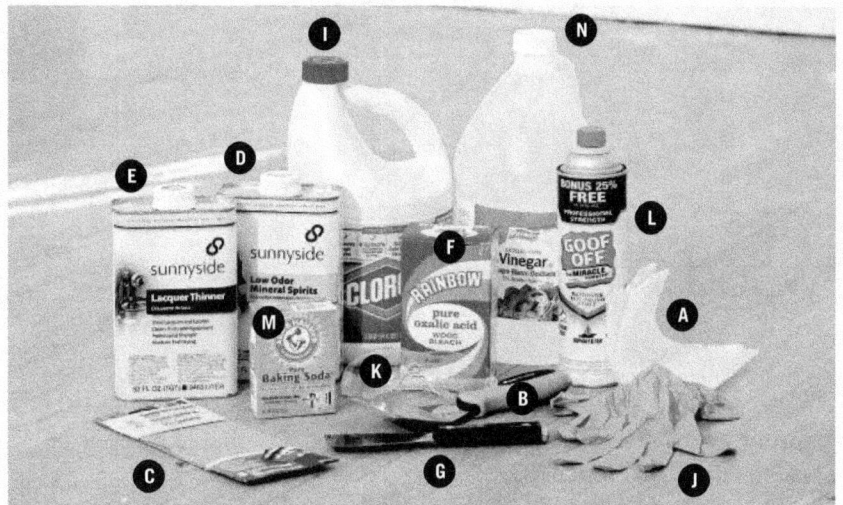

**Products you may need to remove stains from a wood floor include:** extra-fine nylon scrubbing pad (A); sharp scraper (B); sandpaper (C); mineral spirits (D); lacquer thinner (E); oxalic acid (F); putty knife (G); chlorine (I); protective gloves (J); eye protection (K); Goof Off stain remover (L), baking soda (M); vinegar (N).

## How to Use Wood Bleaches

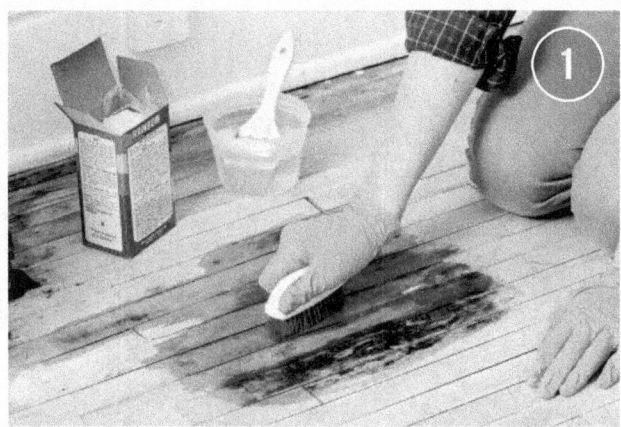

**Choose a bleach appropriate for the stain** (see page 123). Wearing protective gloves, apply the bleach solution to the stain area, being careful to confine it to that area.

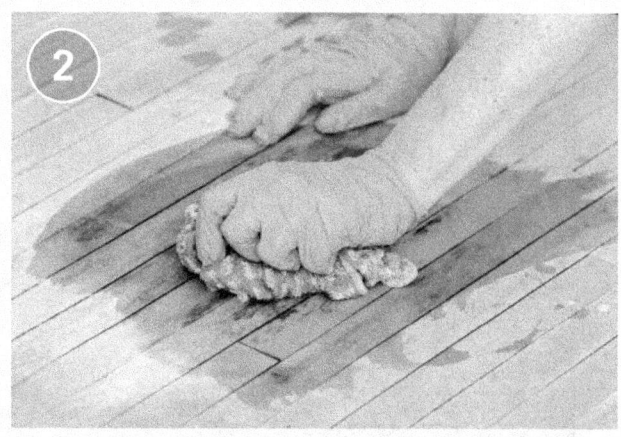

**Let the bleach remain on the stain for the recommended time,** then neutralize the bleach with the recommended agent (baking soda solution for oxalic acid, vinegar solution for household bleach, clear water for Klean Strip). Wash the area thoroughly with clear water, wipe up excess water, and let dry.

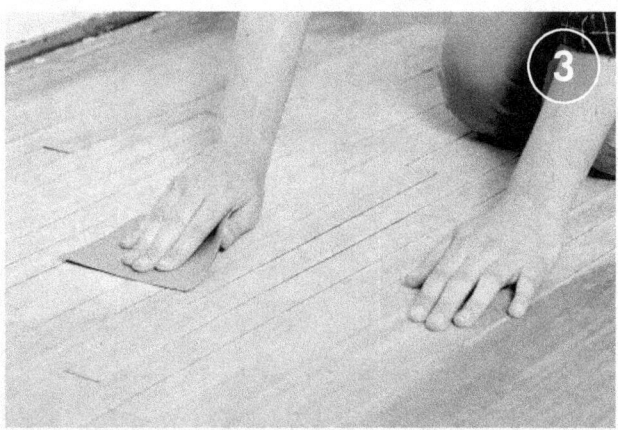

**Once dry, lightly sand the area.** All bleaches will raise the wood grain, and before applying a wood stain, the grain must be sanded smooth.

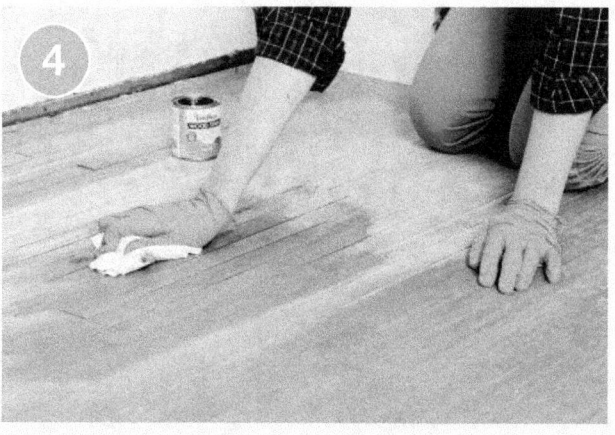

**Apply a rub-on wood stain** that closely matches the tone of the surrounding floor using a soft rag. Let dry completely, then carefully apply a polyurethane or other matching surface finish to blend the stain area with the surrounding floor.

# Refinishing Hardwood Floors

Quality hardwood floors made with solid wood, usually oak or maple, are premier flooring surfaces that have returned to must-have popularity. Whether emerging out from under carpeting, or being renovated after years of use, hardwood is now being proudly displayed again.

There are two ways a hardwood floor can be renovated and before deciding what approach to take, carefully evaluate your floor, because one method is considerably more involved and should be done only if necessary.

The first method is called *screening*—a process that involves fitting an upright floor buffer with a metal screen pad that roughens up the glossy surface finish of your floor without sanding down into the hardwood. After the floor is screened and

all dust removed, a new top finish layer is applied to the floor. Where appropriate, screening and applying a new top coat is a very efficient and relatively easy means to transform a hardwood floor. Screening is appropriate where the wear and damage to a floor is confined to the surface finish, and where the top layer is a standard polyurethane or varnish finish.

But be aware that there are instances where screening and refinishing is not possible. For example, if the floor has been maintained by waxing, or finished with a modern aluminum oxide coat, new polyurethane simply will not bond to the underlying layer, and your only option will be to completely sand down into the wood layer.

The second method for refinishing hardwood is a complete sanding and refinishing project, in which a rented upright drum sander or upright orbital sander grinds down a thin layer of the actual hardwood in preparation for applying a new top coat finish. This is the option if the wood itself shows damage, or if the original top coat is wax or a super-hard aluminum oxide coat. In this method, after the major floor area is sanded with the upright sander, the corners and edges are sanded with a handheld rented edge sander. Historically, this is a difficult project for DIYers, because drum sanders are hard to control and small errors in handling the tool can badly gouge a floor. Careful DIYers can do this successfully.

This project will show you how to evaluate your floor and then give you both options for refinishing: screening to remove just the top surface finish, or complete sanding to remove a thin layer of the actual wood.

**The timeless beauty** of a refinished hardwood floor enlivens the whole room.

# How to Evaluate Your Wood Floors

**First, make sure your floors are solid hardwood** rather than an engineered wood product made from laminated layers of wood. (An engineered wood floor should be sanded only by a professional, since it is all too easy to sand completely through the top layer of wood into the core.) To do this, remove a floor duct or a base shoe molding and look at the flooring material from the side. It should be obvious if the flooring is solid hardwood or a laminated, engineered product.

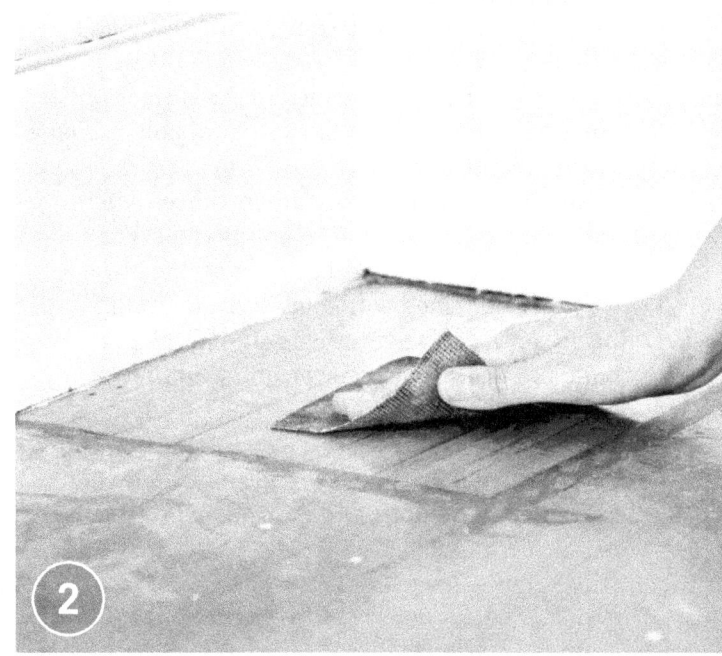

**Evaluate the current surface finish** by taping off a small section in an out-of-the-way place, such as in a closet. Roughen this area with a sanding screen, clean away the dust thoroughly, then brush on a layer of polyurethane finish. Let it dry completely.

**Use a coin to scrape lightly across the dried finish.** If the polyurethane separates and scrapes away easily, the original finish is incompatible with screening and applying a top coat. You will have to deep sand instead.

**Examine the condition of the wood around the room.** If it is in overall good shape except for surface wear to the top coat, your floor is suitable for screening and finishing. But if the wood is badly stained, scratched, or dented, then complete sanding is the better option.

## CHOOSING A POLYURETHANE FINISH

Not all polyurethane finishes are created equal. In general poly finishes for floors are categorized either as oil based (otherwise known as OMU, or Oil Modified Urethane), or water-based polyurethane. Both products are fine for homeowner use, though each has certain advantages. Oil-based finishes tend to have a somewhat amber color, which some people like, and because they are slower to dry, they are more forgiving in terms of allowing surface imperfections to flatten out as they cure. Water-based finishes tend to be very clear, and they dry very quickly and are easy to clean up. The speed with which they dry, however, means they may show surface flaws unless applied with skill. Due to their low odor and easy clean-up, water-based finishes are preferred by most DIYers, while professionals very often lean toward oil-based finishes. Polyurethanes come in various finishes, as well, including satin, semi-gloss, and gloss, depending on the level of shininess you prefer. Polyurethane finishes may be applied over varnished floors but never over shellac, wax, or oil-finished floors. These floors will only accept the same finishes or may be sanded down to bare wood before finishing with polyurethane.

## TIP

**Inspect the floor for nails.** Remove any protruding staples or other obstructions. Nail heads that can be felt should be driven down with a hammer and nail set. Use a scraper or putty knife to remove paint splatter.

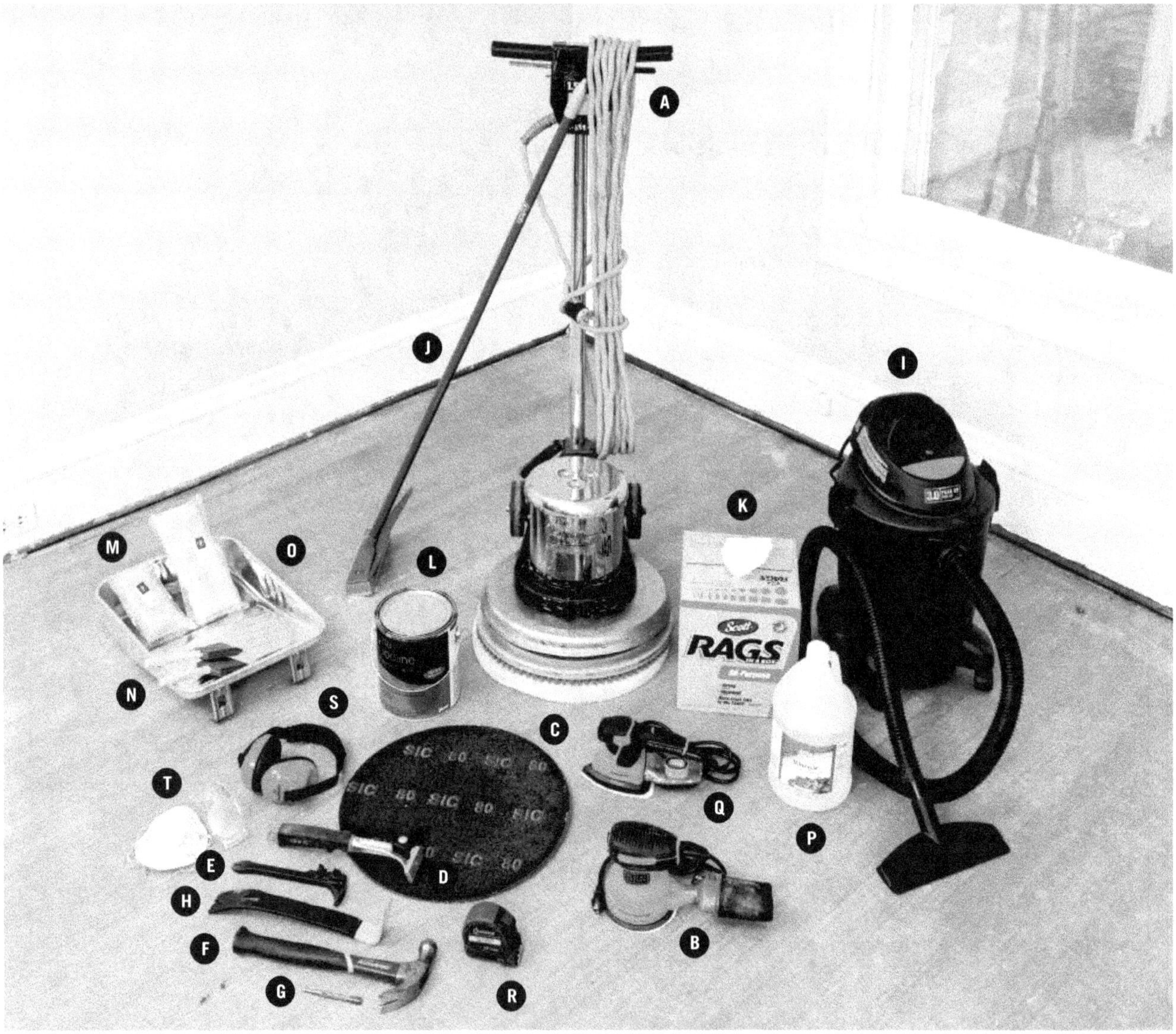

**Tools and materials for screening and refinishing a hardwood floor include:** upright floor buffer (A); handheld random-orbit sander (B); sanding screens for rental sander (C); paint scraper (D); brad puller (E); hammer (F); nail set (G); pry bar (H); shop vacuum (I); mop (J); rags (K); polyurethane finish (L) painting pad (M); paintbrushes (N); paint tray (O), vinegar (P); detail sander (Q); tape measure (R); ear protection (S); particle mask and eye protection (T).

## How to Screen & Refinish a Hardwood Floor

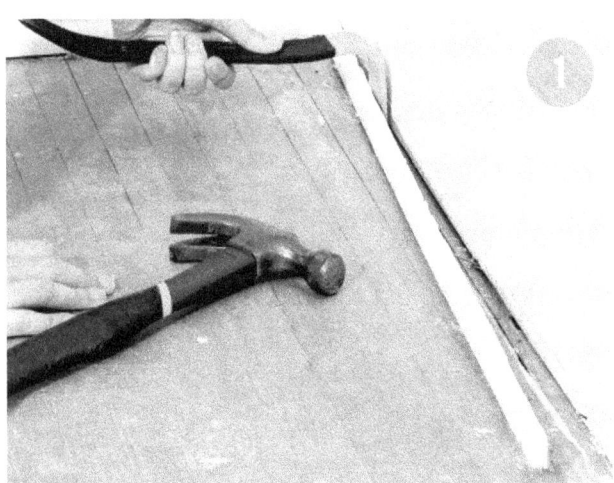

**Remove shoe moldings using a pry bar.** Your results will be best if you screen and refinish all the way to the walls.

**Vacuum floor and damp mop** with a solution of vinegar in water. Make sure to let the floor dry completely, and don't allow standing water to sit on the floor.

**Fit a sanding screen to the bottom** of an upright floor buffer. Buff over the entire floor until the finish is dull and opaque.

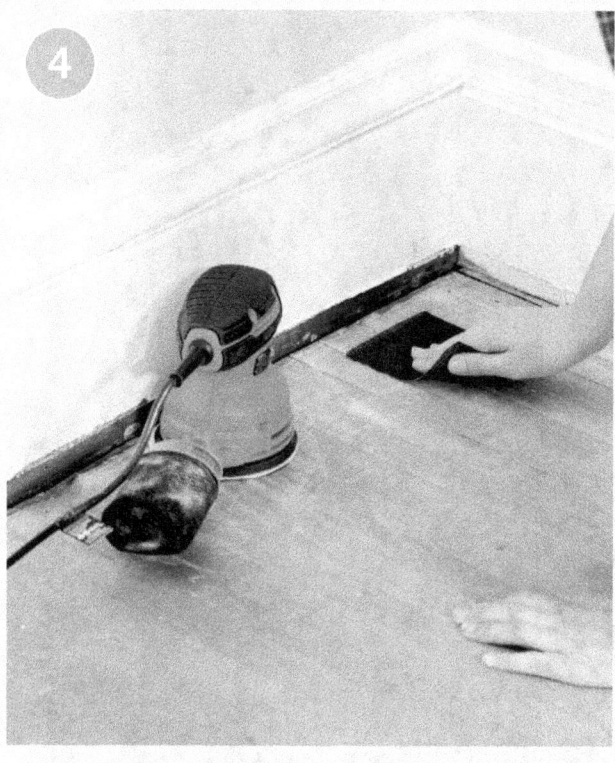

**Screen edges and corners** with a handheld power sander. In the very back of corners, and under obstacles such as radiators, use a piece of sanding screen to remove the finish by hand. Thoroughly vacuum the floor, then wipe it down with a slightly moistened cloth.

**Apply polyurethane finish** as directed by the manufacturer using a painting pad on a pole, and a paintbrush for small corners. If necessary, a second coat can be applied after the first coat dries completely. Lightly buff the previous coat with a fiber pad between coats.

**Reinstall the baseboard moldings.** If the moldings were old and brittle, cutting and installing new pieces may give your floor a nice finishing touch.

**Tools and materials for sanding a hardwood floor include:** hammer (A); nail set (B); sheet plastic (C); painter's tape (D); ear protection (E); drum sander [rented] (F); floor sander/edger (G); under-radiator sander [rented, if needed] (H); shop vacuum (I); wood filler (J); putty knife (K); clean cloths (L); pre-stain conditioner (M); wood stain (N); latex gloves (O); detail sander/mouse (P); eye protection (Q); and respirator (R).

# How to Sand a Hardwood Floor

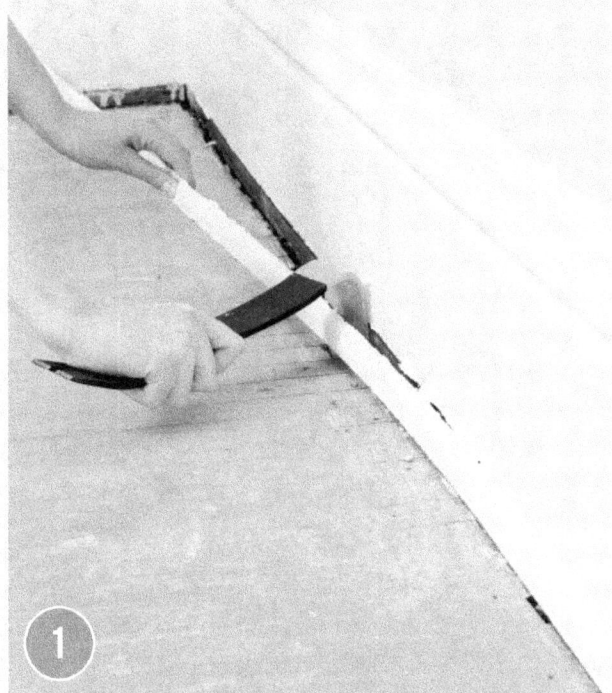

**Examine the floor** and remove any protruding tacks or staples. Drive down any nail heads that can be felt by hand. Scrape away any paint splatters from the floor. Vacuum the floor thoroughly. Damp-mop the floor and let it dry completely.

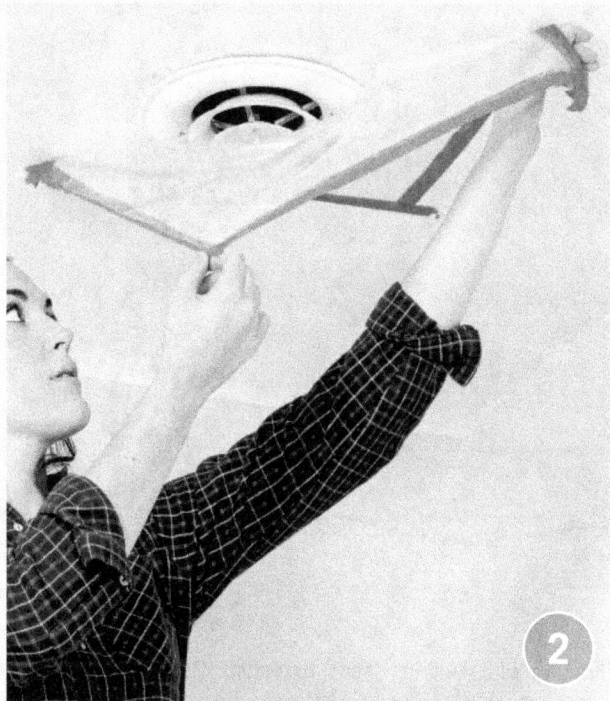

**Cover doorways, HVAC vents, and other openings** with sheets of plastic. Shelves holding books or other decorative items can also be covered with plastic. Power sanding a floor is a messy business, and dust can infiltrate any opening.

**Examine the floor for loose or bowed boards,** and if necessary, nail them down. Badly damaged floorboards should be replaced (see page 144). Examine any stained areas. Surface stains will probably sand out, but deep stains, such as where water damage has soaked in, may require that the floorboards be replaced.

### SAFETY TIP

Even with proper ventilation, inhaling sawdust is a health risk. We recommend getting a respirator for a project like this. If you don't use one, you must at least wear a dust mask. Eye protection is also a must; and you'll thank yourself for buying a good pair of strong work gloves—they make the sander vibrations a little more bearable.

*Important! Always unplug the sander whenever loading or unloading sandpaper.*

*(continued)*

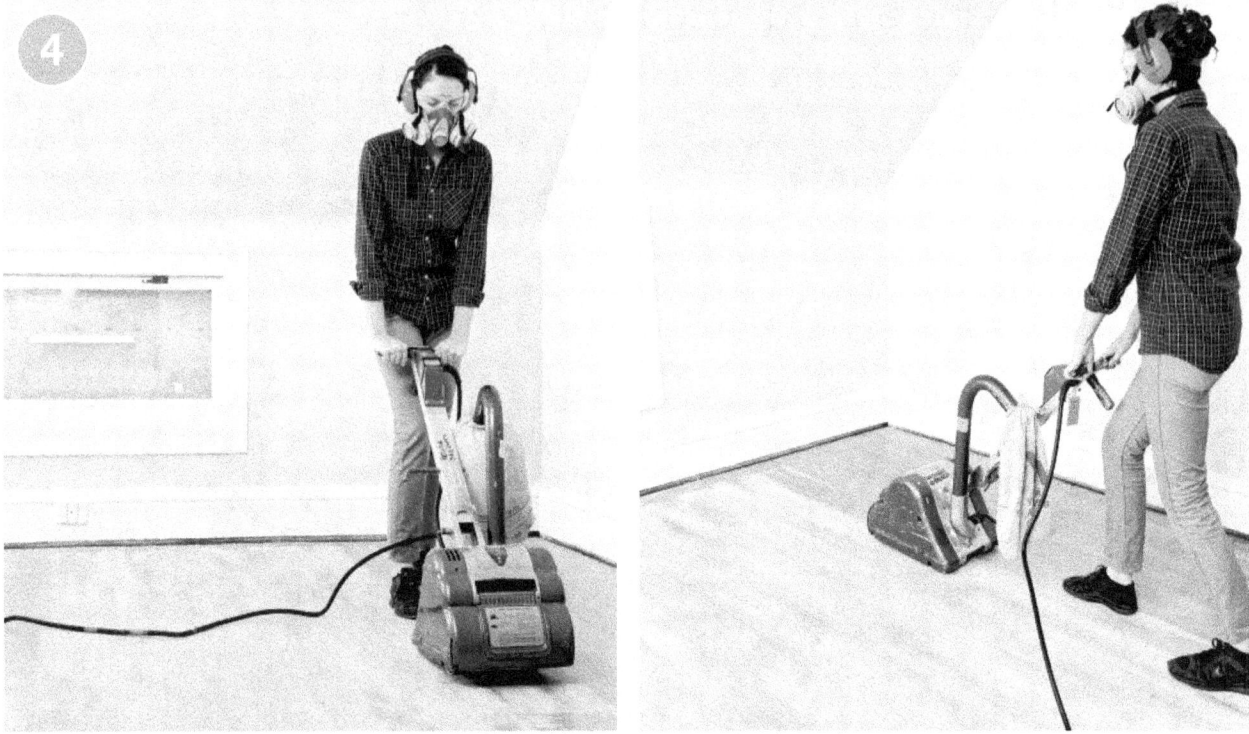

**Practice with the drum sander turned off.** Move forward and backward. Tilt or raise it off the floor a couple of times. A drum sander is heavy, bulky, and awkward. Once it touches the floor, it walks forward; if you stop it, it gouges the floor. For the initial pass with the drum sander, sand with the grain using 40- or 60-grit paper. Start two thirds down the room length on the right side; work your way to the left. Raise drum. Start motor. Slowly lower the drum to the floor and move forward. Lift the sander off the floor when you reach the wall. Move to the left 2" to 4" and then walk it backward the same distance you just walked forward. Repeat.

**In small corners, you may need to sand by hand,** or with a handheld detail sander. After sanding is complete, completely vacuum the floor with a brush attachment.

**Use a paint scraper** to get to corners and hard-to-reach nooks and crannies. Pull the scraper toward you with a steady downward pressure. Pull with the grain. Next, sand with a sanding block.

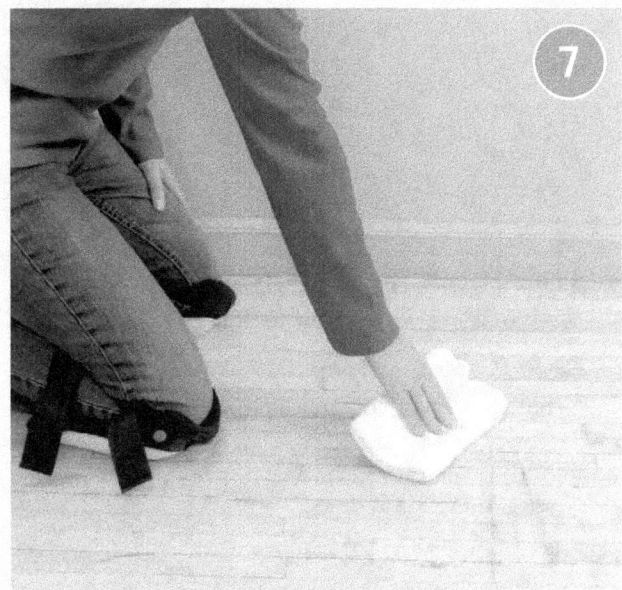

**Prepare the room for finish** by sweeping and vacuuming. Sweep and vacuum again. Wipe up fine particles with a tack cloth.

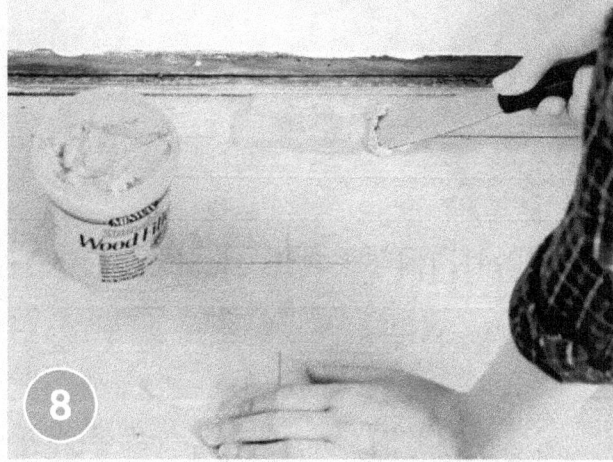

**Examine the floor carefully.** Nicks, knots, holes, or wide cracks between floorboards can be filled with wood filler that color-matches the wood. Let the wood filler dry completely. Repeat steps 4 to 6, first with medium-grit sandpaper, then fine-grit sandpaper. Vacuum thoroughly after each sanding, and after last sanding thoroughly wipe the floor clean with slightly damp (not wet) cloths.

**To stain,** apply the liquid stain to the floor with a brush or clean cloth, in a motion parallel to the wood grain. Allow the stain to soak in for 5 to 15 minutes, then wipe away excess with a clean cloth. If you wish to darken the color, wait about 6 hours, then apply a second coat of stain.

## SANDPAPERS FOR DRUM SANDERS & EDGERS

| Grits | Grade | Use |
| --- | --- | --- |
| 20, 30, 40, 60 | Coarse | To level uneven boards |
| 100, 120 | Medium | To minimize scratches from coarse grits |
| 150, 180 | Fine | To eliminate scratches from medium grits |

Sandpaper becomes less effective over time; it may even rip. Buy three to five sheets of every grade for each room you want to refinish. You won't use them all, but most rentals allow you to return what you don't use. It's far better to have too many than to find yourself unable to continue until the next day because you ran out and the hardware store is closed.

*Reminder: Before you leave the rental shop, have an employee show you how to load the paper. Every machine is a little different.*

# Repairing Scratches & Dents to Hardwood Floors

Although serious physical damage to floorboards requires that they be removed and replaced, most scratches and dents can be repaired. Several methods are possible, depending on the severity of the damage. Remember that on engineered wood floors, the surface layer is usually only 1/16 to 1/8 inches thick. On an engineered hardwood floor, relatively shallow scratches may be enough to expose the core layer, requiring touch-up staining and refinishing, or full replacement.

Serious, deep dents, such as those that occur when heavy tools are dropped on a floor, occur because wood fibers become compressed. If the wood fibers are not broken, dents can often be removed by expanding the wood fibers using heat and moisture.

Whatever repair you attempt, confine your work as narrowly as possible to the damaged area only—the smaller the repair area, the less noticeable it will be.

### TOOLS & MATERIALS

Clean cloths
Odorless mineral spirits
Fine-grit sandpaper
Household iron
Wood filler
Polyurethane finish
Putty knife
Paintbrush
Eye and ear protection
Rubber gloves
Work gloves

## How to Repair Shallow Scratches

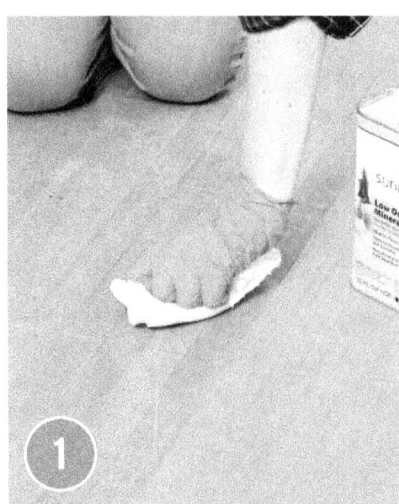

**Sweep the floor clean,** then wash the area around the scratch with a cloth moistened with odorless mineral spirits. Let the floor dry.

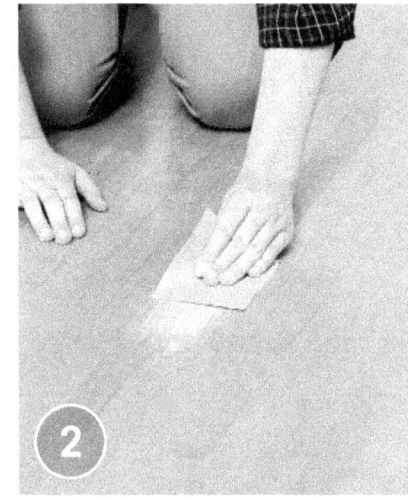

**Lightly sand the scratched area,** sanding parallel to the wood grain, periodically wiping away the sanding dust. It is possible that light sanding will remove the scratch if the damage is only in the surface finish.

**After the scratch is removed,** clean the area with mineral spirits, let dry, and lightly touch up the surface with the same finish used on the rest of the floor, restoring its shine. Be aware that on engineered wood floors, even light sanding may penetrate to the core layer. If so, continue to the directions for deep scratches.

## How to Repair Deep Scratches

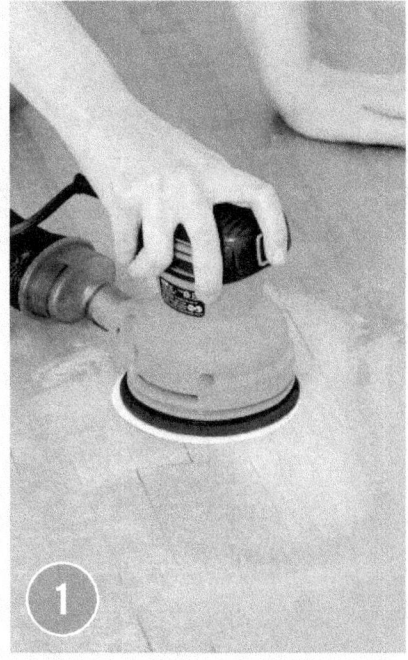

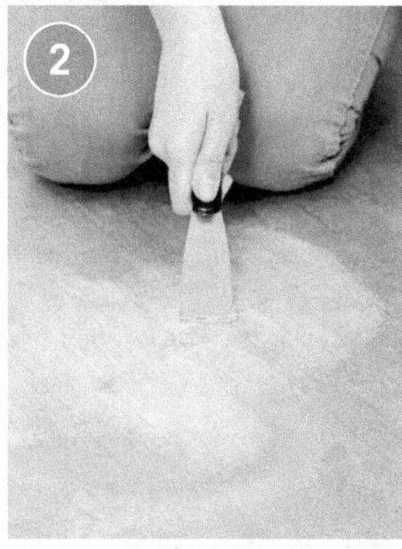

**Clean the scratched area with odorless mineral spirits,** then lightly sand away the surface finish down to bare wood.

**When the bare wood is exposed,** carefully apply a nonwax wood filler to the crack. Colored wood fillers may be available that closely match the color of your floor. If not, you can apply an uncolored wood filler, then stain it to match the floor.

**After the filler dries, lightly sand it.** Wipe away all dust, then apply a rub-on wood stain with a small brush, if needed. Let dry, then apply a surface finish that matches the rest of the floor to the repaired area.

## How to Repair Dents

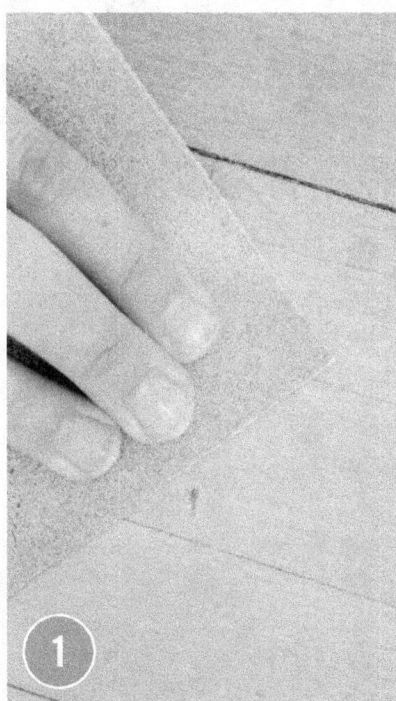

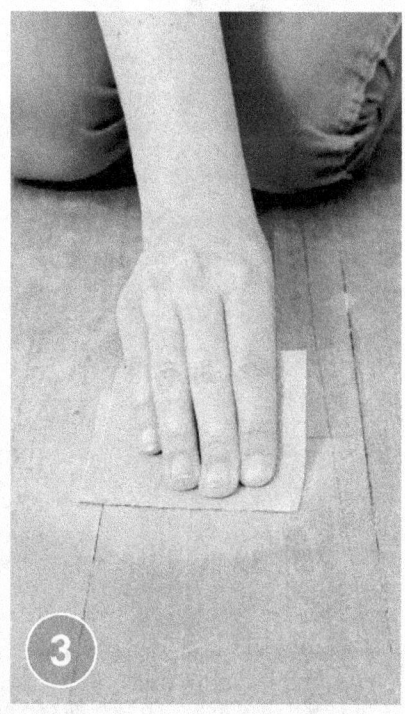

**Clean the area around the dent,** then sand the dented area with fine sandpaper to completely remove the surface finish down to bare wood.

**Moisten the tip of a clean cloth with water,** and place it over the dent. Apply the hot tip of a household clothes iron over the wet cloth, moving it around to drive moisture down into the wood fibers. Try to avoid steaming the surrounding wood finish, as it may discolor it. The dented area should soon swell back, eliminating the dent.

**Let the wood dry completely overnight.** Sand the area lightly, remove the dust, and carefully apply a surface coat of whatever finish covers the rest of the floor.

MAINTAINING WOOD FLOORS • 141

# Fixing Loose & Squeaky Floorboards

Loose floorboards can be as obvious as sections of hardwood or laminated flooring that have visibly buckled, or as subtle as a faint squeak that is heard when you walk over areas of the floor. The squeaks can occur because the surface flooring is loose and pieces are rubbing against one another, or because the subfloor is flexing and rubbing against framing members, or against pipes or ductwork. The following tips are presented in order of complexity. Always start with the easiest potential solution.

### TOOLS & MATERIALS

| | |
|---|---|
| Hammer | Drill |
| Nail set | Wood screws |
| Wood shims | Wood putty |
| Wood glue | Eye protection |
| Construction adhesive | Work gloves |
| Finish nails | |

## Solutions for Loose Floorboards

**The surest way to reattach loose or buckled floorboards** is above. Start by drilling pilot holes for several flooring nails in the floorboard only. The nail will grip better if you do not predrill the wood underlayment and subfloor.

**Existing flooring nails** may have simply loosened from the underlying subfloor, allowing the floor to buckle upward. Look for nail heads securing the flooring, and use a nail set to drive them back down into the subfloor. If the nails are hidden in the tongue-and-groove joints, drill pilot holes on the loose floorboards, and drive finish nails down into the subfloor. Recess the nail heads with a nail set, then fill the holes with wood putty.

# Solutions for Squeaky Floors

**First, find the source of the squeak, if possible.** Have a helper walk back and forth across the squeaky area while you observe from below (hopefully, you have access to the floor from below). If you can see flexing of the subfloor, this is likely the cause of the squeak.

**Look for gaps between subfloor and joists.** Fill these areas with shims glued into place (left), or with construction adhesive that will dry hard and eliminate the space for movement (right). This method also works if you spot areas where the subfloor is flexing and rubbing against pipes or HVAC ducts.

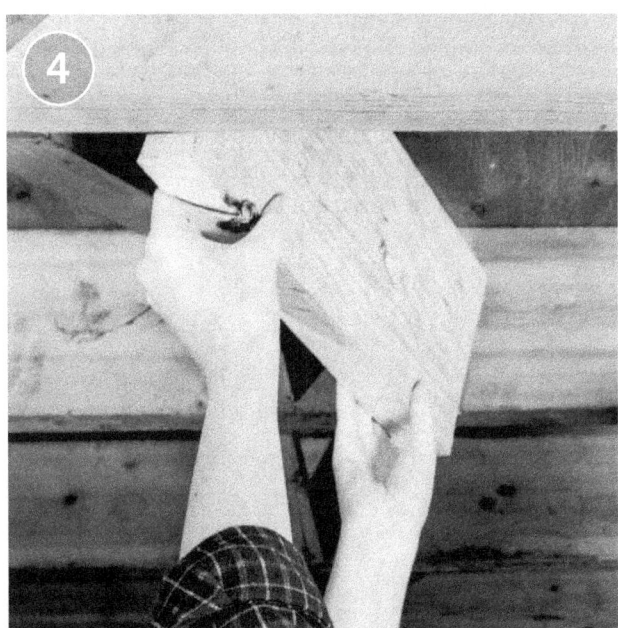

**Installing solid cross-blocking between joists** may also reinforce the floor and eliminate the squeak by eliminating flexing. Apply a bead of construction adhesive along the top of the blocking, then toenail it to the adjoining joists so it is flush up against the subfloor.

**The squeaking may also be caused by gaps** between the surface flooring and the subfloor. As the surface flooring flexes underfoot, the flooring pieces may rub against one another, causing the squeak. The solution here will be to drive screws from below, drawing down the surface flooring and snugging it up against the subfloor. Be careful here, especially with engineered floors, as it is all too easy to drive the screws all the way up though the flooring, leaving exposed screw tips.

# Replacing Damaged Floorboards

There will be instances in which flooring boards are too badly damaged or stained to be repaired with acceptable results. On very deep scratches or dents, it may be impossible to sand out the damage without leaving a noticeable dip. But what if flooring boards have suffered an impact that splintered them beyond repair, or deep water stains or stains from pet urine that are so deep that there's no effective way to remove the stains? In these instances, replacing the boards will be the best option, and in most cases it will be possible to do this in a way that makes the repair invisible to all but the keenest eye.

On a solid hardwood floor, a very good time to replace floorboards is when you are already planning on a deep sanding and refinishing. Once the replaced flooring is installed, a complete sanding down to bare wood will nicely blend in the original floor with the new replacement boards.

Whenever possible, hardwood boards should be replaced along their entire length, not just patched in as a short segment. A replacement board running full length and matching the pattern of the other boards will be almost invisible, especially if the entire floor is being refinished. Where this is not possible, you can outline the damaged area, cut it away with a circular saw and chisel, and cut a tight-fitting replacement piece to insert in the space.

On a laminate floating plank floor, it may easily be possible to lift up and disassemble the entire flooring job back to the damaged board, then reinstall using a replacement board. If this isn't possible, a section of board can be cut out and replaced, although this repair will likely be somewhat visible.

## TOOLS & MATERIALS

**For replacing hardwood planks**
- Eye & ear protection
- Carpenter's square
- Ruler
- Painter's tape
- Drill with spade bit
- Hammer
- Wood chisel
- Small pry bar
- Oscillating multi-tool
- Mallet
- Circular saw
- Nails
- Scrap wood
- Nail set
- Replacement planks
- Wood putty
- Putty knife
- 8d finish nails
- Sandpaper

**For replacing laminate planks**
- Chisel
- Hammer
- Flat pry bar
- Replacement planks
- Nail set
- Finish nails
- Wood putty
- Drill
- Straightedge
- Painter's tape
- Circular saw
- Vacuum
- Eye & ear protection
- Pliers
- Clamps
- Router
- Sandpaper
- Laminate glue
- Wax paper
- Towel
- Weights
- Work gloves

# How to Replace a Full Hardwood Plank

**Use an oscillating multi-tool** to cut the end of a hardwood plank.

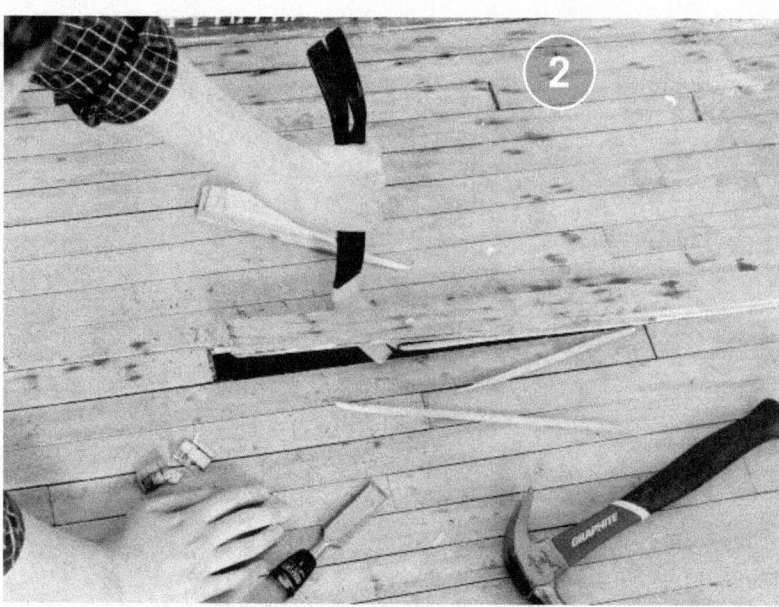

**Use a chisel to pry out the flooring pieces,** and to complete the cuts at the end of the board. Remove any exposed nails visible in the cutout area.

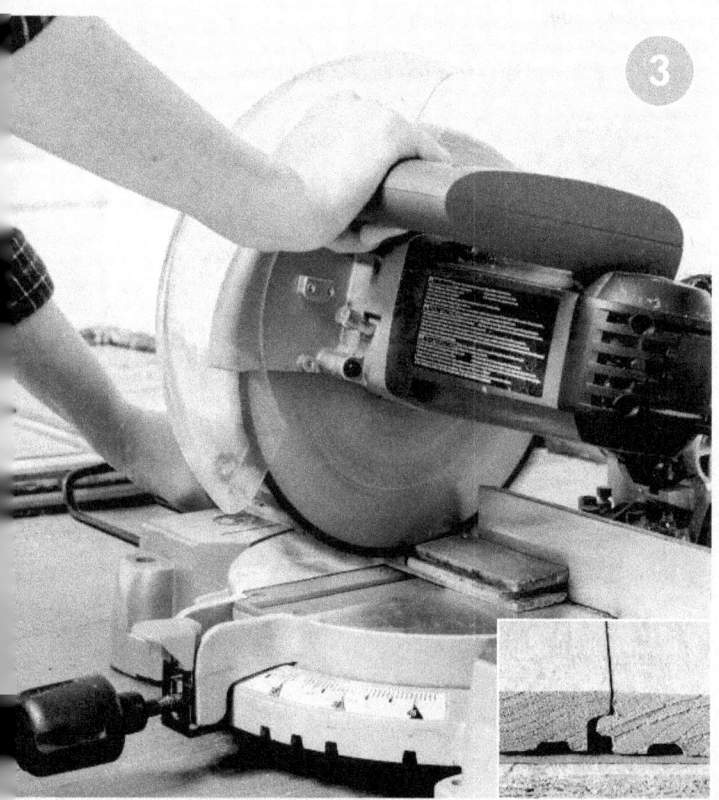

**Cut a new flooring board to length.** Then, use a circular saw, table saw, or wood chisel to cut away the bottom lip of the board's groove. Insert the tongue edge of the new board into the groove of the existing board, and lever the board down into place, so that the remaining top groove edge fits over the tongue of the board at the other side of the cutout, as shown in the inset photo.

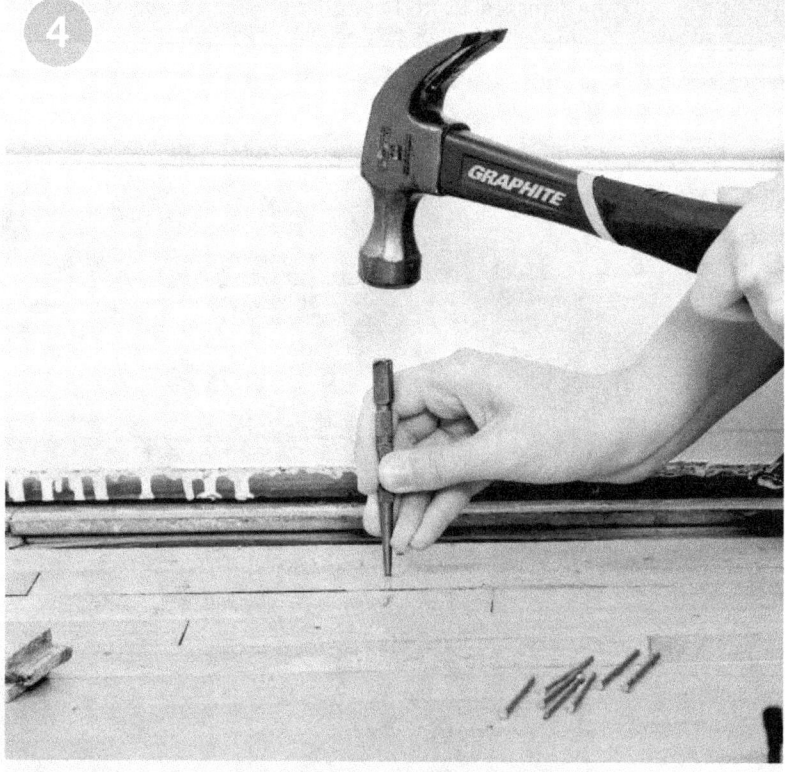

**Facenail the new board in place** by drilling pilot holes and driving finish nails down through the replacement board and into the subfloor. Recess the nail heads with a nail set, and fill the nail holes with putty. Finish the new board with stain and top coat finish to match the rest of the floor.

# How to Replace a Section of Hardwood Flooring

**Use a straightedge to outline cut lines within the boundaries** of the damaged board. To avoid nails, keep the outline at least ¼" inside the seams between boards.

**Drill a hole through the damaged board,** using a spade bit. Drill until you can see the top of the subfloor. Measure the thickness of the floorboard, then set your circular saw to this depth.

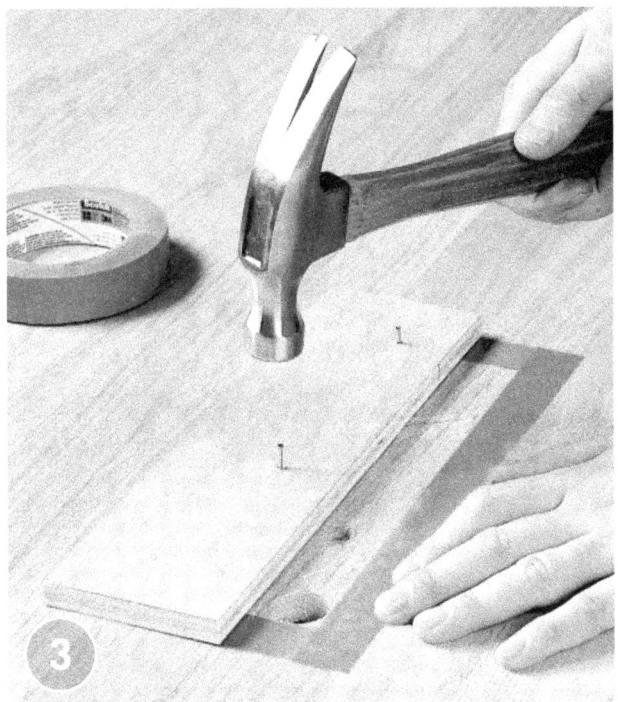

**To prevent the boards from chipping,** place painter's tape along the outside of the pencil lines. To create a straightedge guide for your saw, tack a straight wood scrap inside the damaged area. Set this straightedge guide back from the cutting line a distance equal to the measurement between the saw blade and the edge of the saw foot plate.

**Align the circular saw at an angle** so the front of the saw foot is against the straightedge guide. Turn on the saw, lower the blade into the wood, and cut along the cutting line, stopping ¼" from the corners. Remove the straightedge guide and repeat with other cutting lines.

**Complete the cuts with a sharp chisel** to loosen the damaged board from the subfloor. For clean cuts, the chisel's beveled side needs to face the damaged area.

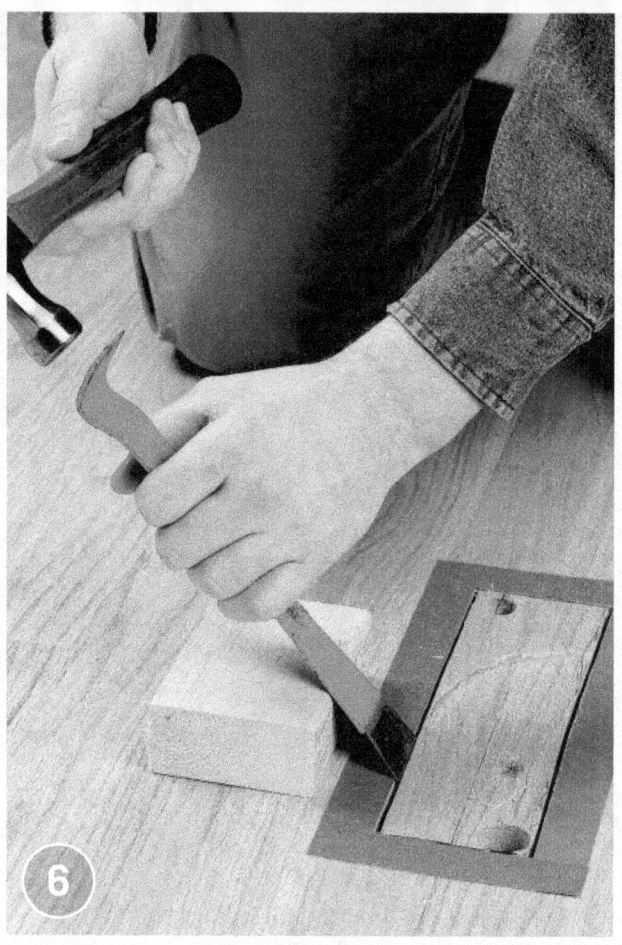

**Using a pry bar, hammer, and 2 × 4 leverage block,** pry up the split board. Remove any nails showing.

**Use the chisel** to remove the narrow strips of remaining wood between the cutout area and the adjoining flooring boards. For a good fit of the replacement board, it is very important to make these cuts as square as possible.

*(continued)*

**Cut a segment of new flooring board to length,** then use the circular saw to cut away the lower lip of the groove on one side of the board.

**Hook the tongue of the replacement piece** into the exposed groove of the adjoining old floorboard and use a rubber mallet to tap the groove side down until it is flush with the surrounding floor.

**On the face of the replacement board,** drill pilot holes angled outward at each end, about ½" from the ends. Drive 1½" 8d finish nails into the pilot holes, securing the repair board to the adjoining floorboards. Recess the nail heads with a nail set, and fill the nail holes with wood putty. If there are any gaps along the edges of the replacement piece, also fill them with wood putty.

**Once the putty is dry,** sand the putty and patch area smooth with fine-grit sandpaper. Sand the edge of the repair board so that the surface is feathered smooth with the adjoining boards. Apply matching wood stain, and let dry; then apply two coats of matching finish. To find out what type of finish your floor has, see page 132.

# How to Replace a Damaged Laminate Plank

**Remove the shoe molding** along the wall side nearest the damaged plank using a chisel or small pry bar. Also remove the moldings along the adjoining walls.

**Use a pry bar** to lift the first board against the wall up and out, and disengage it from the rest of the floor. Continue removing flooring planks until you reach the damaged plank.

**Snap in a replacement plank,** then begin reattaching planks, working backward until you reach the wall where you started.

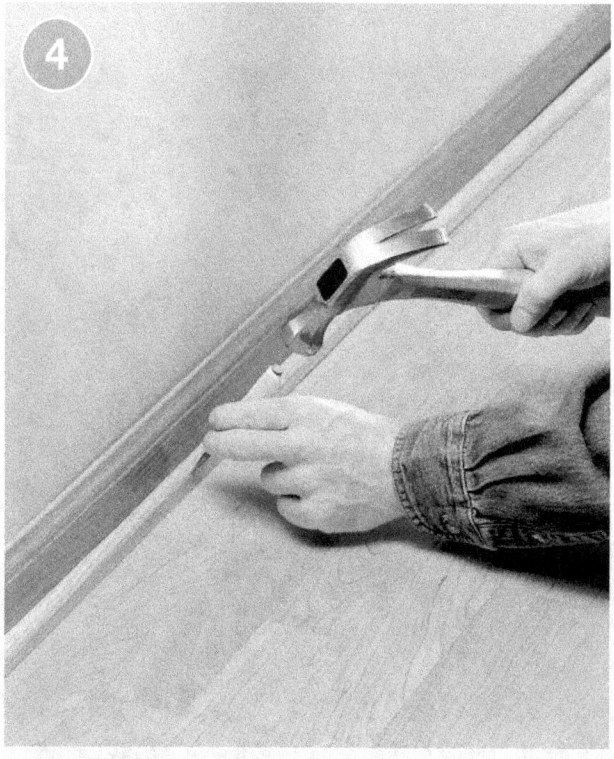

**Reattach the shoe moldings** along the wall using a nail set to countersink finish nails every 6 to 12" along the wall. Fill the nail holes with wood putty.

## How to Replace a Section of Laminate Plank

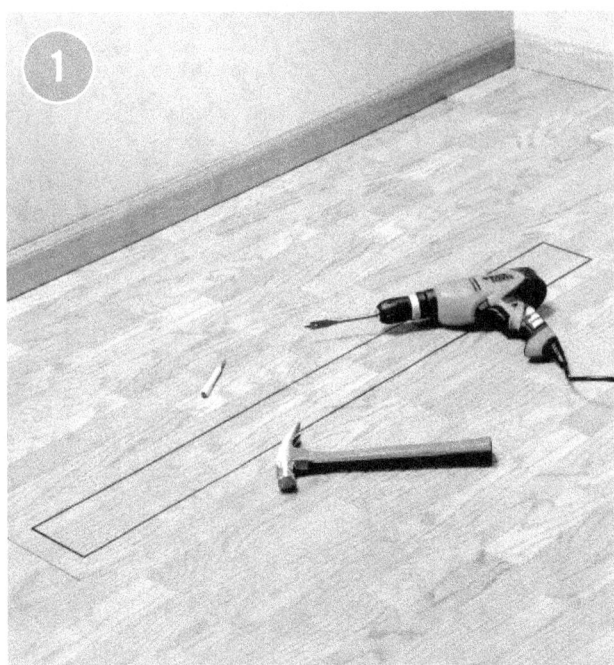

**Draw a rectangle within the boundaries of the damaged board** using a pencil and straightedge. Make sure the rectangle is about 1½" from the edges of the full board. At the corners of the outline, and at the factory corners of the full, drill ⅜" holes down through the blank, just to the subfloor.

**To protect the floor, place painter's tape** along the cutting lines. Set the circular saw blade depth to the thickness of the flooring. Hold the saw at an angle with the front of the saw foot on the floor, then turn on the saw and slowly lower the blade down into the flooring so the blade is aligned with the cutting line. Cut along all cutting lines, but stop ¼" short of the corners. Use a sharp chisel to complete the cuts at the corners of all the drilled holes.

**Lift out the cutout section of flooring,** then use a pry bar and channel-type pliers to lever out and remove the narrow, 1½" strips of flooring still attached to the adjoining planks.

**If the planks were secured with glue,** then use the chisel to remove dried glue from the factory edges of the adjoining planks. Vacuum the cutout area to remove glue flakes and wood chips.

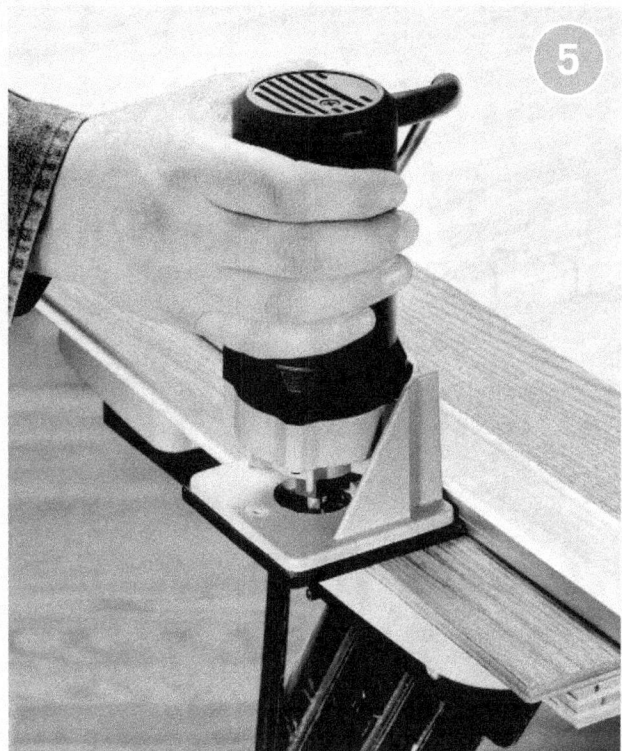

**Remove the tongues on one long edge and one short end** of the replacement plank. The easiest and most accurate way to do this is with a router and straight bit, running the foot of the tool along a clamped straightedge guide. After removal, lightly sand the edge with fine-grit sandpaper.

**Test-fit the replacement board,** sliding the grooves over the tongues on the adjoining boards. Press the plank down into place; if it fits snugly, proceed to the next step. If it does not fit perfectly, then remove the board and lightly sand the edge until the plank fits perfectly.

**Apply laminate glue to the edges of the replacement plank** and into the grooves of the adjoining plank. Press the replacement plank firmly down into place.

**Clean up excess glue with a damp cloth.** Place a strip of wax paper over the replacement plank, the weight down the plank with heavy objects, such as books, evenly distributed over the wax paper. Let the adhesive dry overnight.

# Replacing a Damaged Stair Tread

Minor damage to a stairway tread board can be handled in the same way as other damage to a hardwood floor, as described in previous projects in this chapter. But a tread that is badly cracked or splintered should be replaced entirely.

In many stairways, this is a simple matter of prying up the old tread with a pry bar and installing a matching replacement. But some stairways, especially in newer homes, are built as a prefabricated unit offsite, and the parts are joined together in more complex ways. With these stairs, the process can be more complicated, requiring you to cut the tread into pieces in order to remove it.

### TOOLS & MATERIALS

Pry bar

Oscillating multi-tool

Chisel

Hammer

Cloths

8d finish nails

Nail set

Drill and twist bits

Wood stain

Polyurethane finish

Foam brushes

Eye and ear protection

Work gloves

**Hardwood stair treads** are the highlight of any staircase.

# How to Replace a Hardwood Stair Tread

**If the tread has moldings finishing the edges,** carefully pry these away with a small pry bar.

**Attempt to pry the tread away intact** by driving a pry bar between the tread and the support stringers. On most stairways, the stringers will be located on the ends and in the center of the stairway. You may be able to identify the stringer locations by locating where the nails have been driven to attach the tread.

**If the tread does not come up easily,** as may be the case if the construction has the treads boxed in on the sides, use an oscillating multi-tool to cut between the tread and the wall or molding.

**Lever out the pieces of the tread with a pry bar,** and where necessary, use a sharp chisel to complete the removal at the sides and back of the tread.

*(continued)*

**Buy a matching stair tread.** Standard stairway treads may be available at major home improvement centers or millwork stores. If the proper profile is not available, you may be able to create your own by shaping the proper-sized stock with a router. Cut the tread to the proper length. If the tread is finished with side moldings, you can cut the tread short by ¼" or so to make installation easier.

**Drill pilot holes** through the tread at the stringer locations. Two or three nails per tread should be enough; the pilot holes should be slightly smaller in diameter than the 8d finish nails. Position the tread in place, tight against the back riser. Drive 8d finish nails into each pilot hole, and drive the nail heads below the wood surface with a nail set.

**Apply a top coat finish** to match the rest of the stairs. Let dry completely, then reinstall any trim moldings.

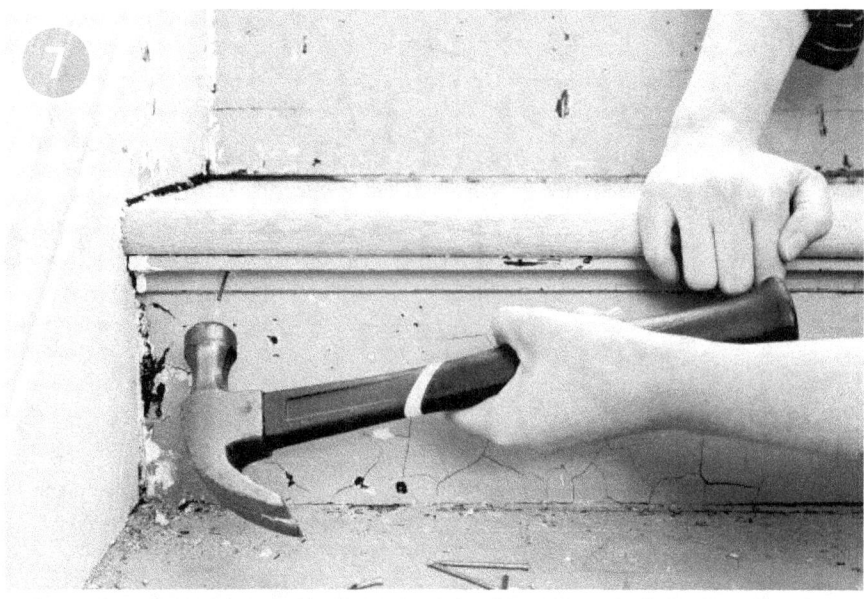

# Metric Conversion Charts

## CONVERTING MEASUREMENTS

| TO CONVERT: | TO: | MULTIPLY BY: |
|---|---|---|
| Inches | Millimeters | 25.4 |
| Inches | Centimeters | 2.54 |
| Feet | Meters | 0.305 |
| Yards | Meters | 0.914 |
| Square inches | Square centimeters | 6.45 |
| Square feet | Square meters | 0.093 |
| Square yards | Square meters | 0.836 |
| Cubic inches | Cubic centimeters | 16.4 |
| Cubic feet | Cubic meters | 0.0283 |
| Cubic yards | Cubic meters | 0.765 |
| Pounds | Kilograms | 0.454 |

| TO CONVERT: | TO: | MULTIPLY BY: |
|---|---|---|
| Millimeters | Inches | 0.039 |
| Centimeters | Inches | 0.394 |
| Meters | Feet | 3.28 |
| Meters | Yards | 1.09 |
| Square centimeters | Square inches | 0.155 |
| Square meters | Square feet | 10.8 |
| Square meters | Square yards | 1.2 |
| Cubic centimeters | Cubic inches | 0.061 |
| Cubic meters | Cubic feet | 35.3 |
| Cubic meters | Cubic yards | 1.31 |
| Kilograms | Pounds | 2.2 |

## LUMBER DIMENSIONS

| NOMINAL - U.S. | ACTUAL - U.S. (IN INCHES) | METRIC |
|---|---|---|
| 1 × 2 | ¾ × 1½ | 19 × 38 mm |
| 1 × 3 | ¾ × 2½ | 19 × 64 mm |
| 1 × 4 | ¾ × 3½ | 19 × 89 mm |
| 1 × 6 | ¾ × 5½ | 19 × 140 mm |
| 1 × 8 | ¾ × 7¼ | 19 × 184 mm |
| 1 × 10 | ¾ × 9¼ | 19 × 235 mm |
| 1 × 12 | ¾ × 11¼ | 19 × 286 mm |
| 2 × 2 | 1½ × 1½ | 38 × 38 mm |
| 2 × 3 | 1½ × 2½ | 38 × 64 mm |

| NOMINAL - U.S. | ACTUAL - U.S. (IN INCHES) | METRIC |
|---|---|---|
| 2 × 4 | 1½ × 3½ | 38 × 89 mm |
| 2 × 6 | 1½ × 5½ | 38 × 140 mm |
| 2 × 8 | 1½ × 7¼ | 38 × 184 mm |
| 2 × 10 | 1½ × 9¼ | 38 × 235 mm |
| 2 × 12 | 1½ × 11¼ | 38 × 286 mm |
| 4 × 4 | 3½ × 3½ | 89 × 89 mm |
| 4 × 6 | 3½ × 5½ | 89 × 140 mm |
| 6 × 6 | 5½ × 5½ | 140 × 140 mm |
| 8 × 8 | 7¼ × 7¼ | 184 × 184 mm |

## METRIC PLYWOOD

| STANDARD SHEATHING GRADE | SANDED GRADE |
|---|---|
| 7.5 mm (5⁄16") | 6 mm (4⁄17") |
| 9.5 mm (3⁄8") | 8 mm (5⁄16") |
| 12.5 mm (½") | 11 mm (7⁄16") |
| 15.5 mm (5⁄8") | 14 mm (9⁄16") |
| 18.5 mm (¾") | 17 mm (2⁄3") |
| 20.5 mm (13⁄16") | 19 mm (¾") |
| 22.5 mm (7⁄8") | 21 mm (13⁄16") |
| 25.5 mm (1") | 24 mm (15⁄16") |

## COUNTERBORE, SHANK & PILOT HOLE DIAMETERS (INCHES)

| SCREW SIZE | COUNTERBORE DIAMETER FOR SCREW HEAD | CLEARANCE HOLE FOR SCREW SHANK | PILOT HOLE DIAMETER HARD WOOD | PILOT HOLE DIAMETER SOFT WOOD |
|---|---|---|---|---|
| #1 | .146 (9⁄64) | 5⁄64 | 3⁄64 | 1⁄32 |
| #2 | ¼ | 3⁄32 | 3⁄64 | 1⁄32 |
| #3 | ¼ | 7⁄64 | 1⁄16 | 3⁄64 |
| #4 | ¼ | 1⁄8 | 1⁄16 | 3⁄64 |
| #5 | ¼ | 1⁄8 | 5⁄64 | 1⁄16 |
| #6 | 5⁄16 | 9⁄64 | 3⁄32 | 5⁄64 |
| #7 | 5⁄16 | 5⁄32 | 3⁄32 | 5⁄64 |
| #8 | 3⁄8 | 11⁄64 | 1⁄8 | 3⁄32 |
| #9 | 3⁄8 | 11⁄64 | 1⁄8 | 3⁄32 |
| #10 | 3⁄8 | 3⁄16 | 1⁄8 | 7⁄64 |
| #11 | ½ | 3⁄16 | 5⁄32 | 9⁄64 |
| #12 | ½ | 7⁄32 | 9⁄64 | 1⁄8 |

# Index

Abrasion Criteria (AC) ratings, 31
adhesive, as part of floor, 23
asbestos, 39, 44

bamboo
  about, 74
  design ideas, 17
  room temperature and humidity, 74
  strip flooring installation
    acclimating, 76
    floor preparation, 76–77
    laying flooring, 77–79
  *See also* maintenance; repair
baseboards
  built-up, 108–109
  one-piece, 106–107
  removal of, 40
Brazilian teak, 30, 31
buffing, 118, 119

carpet
  evaluating existing, 27
  removal of, 38, 43
  transitions to, 58–59
ceramic tile
  evaluating existing, 26–27
  removal of, 38, 42
  underlayment and, 45
chemical strippers, 24

color
  as design element, 34
  distressed floors and, 117
concrete flooring
  cleaning, 63
  evaluating existing, 27
  subfloor panel installation over, 48–51
  *See also* floor leveler
counterbores, plugging, 69
Cumaru (Brazilian teak), 30, 31

dents, 141
design elements
  color, 34
  finish, 31
  pattern, 32–33
  size of elements, 33
  texture, 34
design ideas
  distressed finishes, 117
  floor types, 9–17
  for stains, 115
door casings, 63

end-grain wood tiles
  about, 104
  design ideas, 15
  installation, 105

engineered flooring
  concrete flooring and, 27
  design ideas, 10, 12, 14, 16, 17
  existing flooring and, 24
  flooring selection, 28–29
  grade level and, 27
  thickness and, 31
  *See also* maintenance; repairs
expansion joints, 63

finishes
  about, 114
  aged, 114, 117
  choosing polyurethane, 133
  as design element, 34
  distressed finish application, 117
  evaluating, 127
  floor maintenance and, 126
  hand-scraped, 11, 16
  oil, 14
  wax, 118–119
  *See also* paint; stains
floor anatomy, 23
floor leveler
  applying, 47
  raised subfloor panels and, 49
flooring removal
  asbestos and, 39
  baseboards, 40
  carpet, 43

ceramic tile, 42
dust containment, 38
resilient tile, 42
sheet vinyl, 41
tools for, 39
underlayment, 44–45
flooring selection
   hardness, 31
   hardwood
      exotic woods, 30
      flooring grades, 29
      odd lots flooring, 29
      solid vs. engineered, 28–29
      thickness, 31
   laminate flooring, 31
Forest Stewardship Council (FSC), 28

grade level, 27

hardness (Janka) scale, 31
hardwood flooring
   chemical strippers, 24
   cleaning with mineral spirits, 24
   cutting, 56
   decorative medallion installation, 96–97
   evaluating existing, 24–25, 27
   exotic flooring, 30
   flooring selection, 28–29
   fully bonded strip, 72–73
   grades of, 29
   installation
      cutting, 56
      overview, 55
      plank floors, 66–71
      tips for, 62–63
      tools for, 57, 63
      wood strip, 72–73
   Janka/hardness scale, 31
   plank flooring
      acclimating, 66
      installation, 66–71
      plugging counterbores, 69
   signs of resanding, 25
   transitions
      floor gaps, 60
      staircases, 61
      thresholds and moldings, 58–59
   uneven, 24
   water damage, 25
   *See also* maintenance; refinishing; repairs; vintage floors
hesquite, 31
hickory, 31

inlayed borders, 14
Ip, 30, 31

Janka scale, 31
joists, 23
   flooring direction and, 66

laminate flooring
   about, 31, 80
   Abrasion Criteria (AC) rating, 31
   concrete flooring and, 27
   cutting around obstacles, 88–89
   existing flooring and, 25
   floating floor installation, 85–87
   floor preparation, 83–84
   grade level and, 27
   installation tools, 82
   sheet underlayment for, 84
   variety of, 82
   wall spacers and, 84
   *See also* maintenance; repairs
linoleum tiles, 26, 42
   *See also* resilient flooring

maintenance
   dent repair, 141
   evaluating finishes, 127
   finish type and, 126
   loose floorboards, 142
   scratches
      repair of deep, 141
      repair of shallow, 140
      type of floor and, 140
   squeaks, 143
   *See also* refinishing; stain removal
maple, 10, 11, 31
measuring, rooms, 35
medallion, decorative, 96–97
mesquite, 31
mineral spirits, for cleaning existing floor, 24
moisture content, 63
molding
   baseboard removal, 40
   built up baseboard, 108–109
   one-piece baseboard, 106–107
   for transitions, 58–59

oak, 12, 14, 31
one-piece base molding, 106–107

paint
- advantages of, 120
- application, 122
- checkerboard application, 123
- dilute, as stain, 114
- floor preparation for, 121–122
- mixing, 122
- primer, 121–122
- sealer, 121
- *See also* finishes; stains

parquet
- about, 92
- design ideas, 12, 13, 92
- diagonal layout installation, 95
- tile installation, 93–95

Patagonian rosewood, 30

pattern, 32–33

pegged plank flooring, 103

planning
- evaluation of existing flooring
  - carpet, 27
  - ceramic tile, 26–27
  - concrete, 27
  - hardwood, 24–25, 27
  - resilient, 26–27
  - subfloor, 27
  - underlayment, 27
  - vinyl/linoleum tiles, 26
- importance of, 21
- planning checklist, 22
- room measurement, 35
- selecting floor type, 22

preparation
- floor leveler, 47
- raised subfloor panel installation, 48–51
- subfloor repair, 46
- underlayment installation, 47

products. *See* tools

radiant heat, bamboo flooring and, 74

raised subfloor panels
- anatomy of, 48
- benefits of, 48
- floor leveler and, 49
- installation over concrete, 49–51

random-width planks, 10, 16

red oak, 31

refinishing
- choosing polyurethane finishes, 133
- evaluating floor condition, 132
- inspection for nails, 133
- sanding
  - process for, 137–139
  - sandpapers for, 139
  - tools for, 136, 139
- screening
  - process for, 134–135
  - tools for, 134
- screening vs. sanding, 130–131

repairs
- floorboard replacement, timing of, 144
- hardwood flooring
  - plank replacement, 145
  - section replacement, 146–147
- laminate flooring
  - damaged plank, 149
  - damaged section, 150–151
- loose floorboards, 142
- squeaks, 143
- stair tread replacement, 152–154

resilient flooring
- evaluating existing, 26–27
- removal of, 42

respirators, 137

safety
- asbestos and, 39, 44
- sanding and, 137

sanding
- process for, 137–138
- safety and, 137
- sandpapers for, 139
- signs of past, 25
- tools for, 136, 139
- vs. screening, 130–131

sandpapers, 139

scratches
- deep, 141
- shallow, 140

screening
- process for, 134–135
- tools for, 134
- vs. sanding, 130–131

sheet vinyl flooring, removal of, 38, 41

Southern pine, 31

squeaks, 143

stain removal
- products for, 129
- types of stains, 128
- wood bleach application, 129

stains
- applying to bare wood, 116
- design ideas, 115
- dilute paint as, 114
- selecting, 114
- *See also* finishes; paint; stain removal

staircases
- tips for, 61
- tread replacement, 152–154

subfloor
- about, 23
- evaluating existing, 27
- hardwood installation and, 62
- raised subfloor panel installation, 48–51
- repairing sections, 46

texture, 34

thresholds
- existing flooring and, 26
- for transitions, 58–59

Tigerwood, 30

tile. *See* ceramic tile; linoleum tile; vinyl tile

tongues and grooves
- milling, 100–101
- routing, 102

tools
- chemical strippers, 24
- for floor removal, 39
- hardwood installation, 57
- for laminate flooring, 82
- mineral spirits, 24
- for sanding, 136, 139
- for screening and refinishing, 134
- for stain removal, 129

underlayment
- ceramic tile and, 45
- evaluating existing, 27
- installing plywood, 47
- removal of, 38, 44–45

vintage floors
- about, 98
- acclimating, 99
- milling tongues and grooves, 100–101
- pegged plank flooring, 103
- reclaiming directly, 99
- routing tongues and grooves, 102

vinyl tile
- evaluating existing, 26
- removal of, 38
- *See also* sheet vinyl flooring

walnut, 31

Wenge, 30, 31

wide planks, design ideas, 12, 14

wood bleaches, 129

wood block flooring. *See* end-grain wood tiles

www.ingramcontent.com/pod-product-compliance
Lightning Source LLC
Chambersburg PA
CBHW081359070526
44583CB00020B/2595